The Wonder of It All

The Wonder of It All

An Old Soldier Remembers

Clarence Sheffield

PROVIDENCE PUBLISHING CORPORATION
FRANKLIN, TENNESSEE

Printed in the United States of America

09 08 07 06 05 1 2 3 4 5

Library of Congress Control Number: 2005921635

ISBN: 1-57736-340-X

Cover design by Hope Seth

Unless otherwise noted, Scripture quotations are taken from the Holy Bible, King James Version, Cambridge, 1769.

HILLSBORO PRESS
an imprint of
Providence Publishing Corporation
238 Seaboard Lane • Franklin, Tennessee 37067
www.providence-publishing.com
800-321-5692

To Six of My Inspirational Teachers

As one could imagine, from first grade through six years of college I sat down and faced many teachers. Only six were pedagogically endowed by the Master of teaching. If a teacher has this endowment, it shows and comes so naturally. We simply cannot pay these teachers what they are worth. These teachers should be teaching teachers—there's nothing like watching these dedicated people teach and then going out and doing likewise.

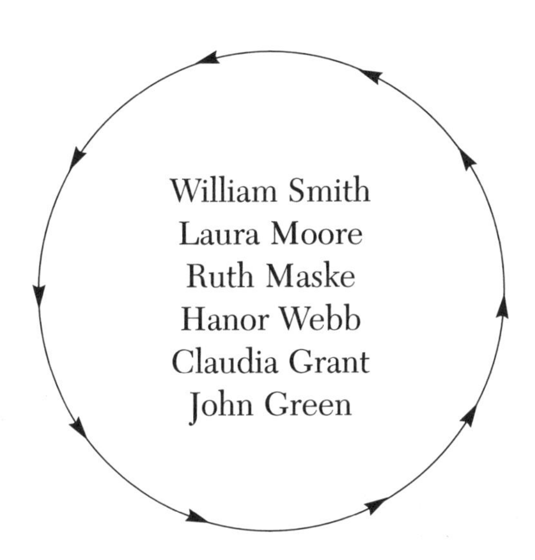

Eternal Movement——Pedagogically Endowed by the Master of Teaching.

The circle and the figures on its line symbolize their never-ending influence as it lives on as the waves on the sea—eternally.

These teachers impacted my life and motivated me in ways I simply can't describe. Don't tell me they are dead, either. They are basking on flower-bedecked banks of the sweet forever. Who do you think I thought about and dreamed about so much as I lay on damp blankets with an ammo metal box for a pillow, watching the stars and wondering if I'd ever see these United States again? Their teachings came to me so frequently and lifted me up, even as we were millions of miles apart. I wanted to be like them so I chose teaching.

Contents

Part 2—The War Years

Part 3—Teaching Years

Part 4—In Retirement

Acknowledgments

Dr. Rose Ann Coleman edited my original writing. She never grew weary of correcting misspelled words or grammar mistakes. She also arranged the chapters in chronological order. I salute her efficient work. The original text was typed by Becky Effler, Fran Nichols, Julie Knestrick, and Booth Kammann. These four typists deserve an "A" for their outstanding work of love and commitment.

Jim Knestrick did the work of sorting out original pictures, organizing them in a portfolio, and indicating the chapters in which they belonged. Shirley Ann Sheffield Green has acted as liaison between Providence House Publishers and me, running back and forth between Nolensville and Cool Springs. This is a big help to me, as I am now eighty-seven years old, and I have needed a chauffeur for some time.

I have been blessed with wonderful encouragers over the long years. My wife Reitha had two terminal diseases: congestive heart failure and emphysema. Yet she was an untiring encourager until the end. March 1, 2004, she was laid to her eternal rest. I have hundreds of other encouragers and well-wishers. I love you, encouragers. I thank you all, as I can't thank you all individually.

Introduction

After being retired twenty-four years as an elementary teacher and principal, I have had many urges lately to put on paper what I think would be of help to my fellow countrymen and thousands of teachers. My days are slipping by rapidly now as my eighty-seventh birthday has come and gone. Over one thousand of the World War II veterans are passing the torch to a newer generation each day. I simply must write some things that are stored up in my heart and mind that need to come out.

For many years I could not do this. The Lord has a way of erasing many horrendous events too difficult to talk or write about. Now as I see movies so graphic like *Saving Private Ryan* and *Pearl Harbor*, many memories in the recollection chamber of my brain are coming back. Those memories, plus a desire that burns within so strongly, compel me to write.

This is my personal belief: we are destined before birth. Our mighty and awesome God knew us long before we were even conceived. Everything was laid out—the way we were to go, but then God gave each a choice. Everyone has free will to choose the higher power, to follow God, to be obedient, and to be a person who is on the road to higher and nobler things. Those who are never happy in their work are bent on making a world of their design and their accomplishments.

This is my story, my memoir. I want to the best of my ability to give my life's story. There are no ulterior motives other than to let the thousands I have taught and many others know what God has done for me personally, to bring glory to His name, and not this mortal.

The Wonder of It All

Part 1

My Childhood

Before Birth Occurrences

Everything said here will depend on what my earthly father told me when I was a very young boy. He was a godly man of integrity and truth.

In 1917, there was a worldwide epidemic of what we called Spanish flu. In most cases this disease was fatal as there was very little medicine to treat it. In the South in late winter and early spring, this contagious disease decimated whole communities. Mother was seven and a half months pregnant with me when she came down with this dreaded flu. Father called our family doctor, Wesley Blair, and he came; what he prescribed, my father did. However, later my father told me that the medicine did no good.

Dad sat up with his pregnant wife four days and nights and gave the medicine. Exhausted, he hitched a horse to the wagon and went to get Mother's only sister, Julie, to help him. Although this put her own life at risk, Aunt Julie came.

Father had a bottle of turpentine, and every morning he and Aunt Julie put a drop of the liquid turpentine on their tongues. He had heard testimonies from the Negro turpentine gatherers that they never got sick, never even had colds, and they attributed their great health to a drop of the liquid touched to the tongue daily.

Whether it was a miracle or God's working through the turpentine, neither my father nor my aunt became ill when so many were dying all around them.

Dr. Wesley Blair came back and told my father to continue giving the medicine to my mother, but that she would be dead before all the medicine was taken. Father told him he had another doctor's opinion for my mother's fate; Dr. Blair demanded to know who this doctor was. Father just held his hand upward toward heaven.

The doctor left. Dad did two things: gave Mother the prescribed medicine and prayed. When all the medicine was taken, she was better. More medicine was ordered, and she survived. A great man of faith, my father prayed, and God heard his prayers and performed a miracle right there in the little community of Mt. Union in the Piney Woods section of south Alabama.

That was in March, and on May 21, 1917, I was born with no health problems other than being smaller than my brothers and sisters had been.

My Parents' Background

I was born into a family of English immigrants who came to America in 1792. My father told us children the Sheffields came from the textile center of Manchester. His remarks were sketchy, and he didn't go into details as much as we hoped he would. I do know the Sheffields came to America seeking more freedom in the realm of religion.

My father's mother was a full-blooded Creek Indian named Fronnie. I faintly remember Grandma. One thing that stands out that I do remember was her great love for all of us. This love was manifested not in what she said but in what she did.

My father's dad, Coleman Sheffield, was a soldier in the Civil War. Everyone called him Coley. His older brother, James, was a colonel in the Confederacy and was killed at Chickamauga. A bronze marker with his name and rank was erected on Highway 27 leading out of Georgia into Chattanooga through the military park.

Clarence with his mother and father before shipping out.

Francis Jane Butler Sheffield, my mother, after having a stroke in her later years, was left senile and confined to a wheelchair, but she was still aware of many things that went on in her everyday life.

Each day at six o'clock a certain very popular news anchor came on television to give the news. Despite the stroke, Mama would smooth out her dress, pat her hair in place, and be ready long before the time came. She could hear and see him, so she thought he could hear and see her. She would get primped up, move close to the screen, smile a lot, and respond to him, as if he were speaking directly to her.

All my relatives on my mother's side were workaholics, and I am a carbon copy of them. The genes do indeed make a difference. She had three brothers and one sister. There are no survivors now.

Mother lived most of her life in Apalachicola, Florida, in Liberty County. Her father died when she was very young. He was in the logging and timber business but liked to fish when not working. She said most of the logs he cut were cypress, and he had to wade in lakes and ponds to cut them. Here is where he met his death. A stingray stung him, and he died before anyone could get him to a doctor.

Evidently Mother had music in her. Although she couldn't read music, she put me to sleep every night playing the song on the organ, "He promised never to leave me, no never to leave me alone." People don't sing now as they did when I was growing up.

Our nearest small village was five miles north of Mt. Union. Our nearest neighboring community was a black community named Needmore. People driving those Model T Fords and Model As would stop and stand amazed and laugh while gazing at the Needmore's city sign.

Later as I was growing up, I realized where I made my entrance into this world was anything but beautiful and pleasing to the eye. I told my parents our community should have been named Needmore; it was more appropriate than Mt. Union.

Forlorn describes Mt. Union perfectly. I looked out on the large expanse of land my parents called their dream as something foreboding and uninviting. When I was a little fellow, all my parents ever did was work and talk about their plans to expand this farm. All I could do for recreation was feed all the chickens.

In 1912, the boll weevil came across the Mexican border into Texas. A few years after this, cotton was no longer king in the South. It proved a blessing in disguise because the presence of the boll weevil forced farmers to diversify. Their efforts were so successful that a monument was raised in Enterprise, Alabama, to the boll weevil.

My father, Wesley Avant Sheffield, stopped raising so much cotton and started with strawberries, soybeans, peanuts, corn, and cattle. After three or four years we bought a Model T Ford as we then had more cash crops. That car was our family's monument to the famous weevil.

I had three brothers and four sisters, Rosa Ann Sheffield Pate, Benny Leon Sheffield, Ellis Lawrence Sheffield, Cassiemae Sheffield Padgett, Evelyn Love Sheffield Wilson, (myself), Wesley Avant Sheffield, and Violet Elsie Sheffield Daffin. I was the sixth child but now am the oldest living member of the Sheffield family. Wesley Jr. was two and a half years younger than I. My only living sister, Violet, lives in Milton, Florida.

The Sheffield family—Clarence is third from left on front row.

While fighting in World War II, Wesley, or W. A., was guarding an ammunition depot at night. W. A. was so badly wounded, he was left as dead. Medics found him. He was on one of the islands. Before his death, Wesley forgave the Japanese, and we are so glad of that.

When we were together, it seemed there was no end to our talking about the war and our precious memories growing up and playing baseball in the good old community of Mt. Union, Alabama.

America started the Civilian Conservation Camps (CCC) in the dark days of the Depression. Older teenage boys were allowed to sign up to go to one of these camps. My brother, W. A. or Dub, went to one of these in Pollock, Louisiana. These boys were paid one dollar per day, plus clothes and food. If I remember correctly, my parents got twenty-five of those every month. That left five for my brother. He never once complained of the ratio he got. These boys were under strict military life. They did close order drills and many necessary lessons a soldier learns. Some of the trainings were about guns and how to conduct inspections.

When we were forced into World War II we at least had a few men who had some training, and they became noncommissioned officers. It was a God-sent blessing. We appreciated what our country did. At times we thanked our country for this foresight. Where there is no vision, people perish.

During my growing up years, families were large. During this era, some parents had their favorite sons and daughters whom they loved more than others. It was true in my family. My mother seemed to love me more than the rest of the family members or siblings. They all knew this. One cannot fool children. My father's favorite son was Wesley, named after him, and we all knew this, too. I was smaller than the rest of the children and was called the runt in my family by some of my siblings.

Even when there is love and good training by parents, some children are cruel and rude to each other, especially if that particular child seems to be the favorite or favored one. I heard comments when Mother and Father weren't around such as, "He will never amount to anything." This had a profound effect on me to rise up and show them! As a result, I was the only member of my family to finish college. I got motivated!

I have never seen nor heard a parent admit this preference for one of his or her children over another. In my long teaching career, I suspected this was happening but never mentioned it. It needs to be said because it is true.

Sometimes this is a cause for sibling rivalry and hard feelings. We need to practice and promote harmony, peace, love, and caring for each other. One thing that helped my family was all of us sitting down at the table at the same time, giving thanks, and eating together. It seems as if eating together causes a family to cling together.

Today, the family seems to illustrate centrifugal force of a wheel turning when it comes to eating together. All things on the wheel are slung off in all directions. On the other hand, when all sit down together, centripetal force is illustrated. When the old clock is wound, the spring gets tighter and closer together. So does the family.

Wesley was with my father when he drew his last breath, the only child there. My father died in the arms of his favorite son. My youngest brother said, "Father came up from the bed saying, 'I see you, Lord, come on and get me; I am ready.'" In an instant he was gone.

Trying to Keep the Wolf from the Door

Because we were poor, every member of our family was aware that we all had to work hard and ask God to bless our labors if we were to survive during the Depression. We planted our crops and then a warm rain came—in a few days, it looked as if every seed that was planted came up. Our country was still in an agricultural economy. We could see our dependence on our all-wise and merciful heavenly Father. All of this hard work and dependence on Him taught us that God was a supreme being and worthy of praise and worship. In our final assessment of the situation, we concluded that through difficulty, and only through difficulty, there is growth.

I have thanked God many times for letting me live during my allotted time and beyond. I have done things that I could not do today that were good for my children and the society in which we are living. God has a time laid out for each of us if only we will keep an open ear and receptive heart to the wooing of the Holy Spirit. We can be the voice of Jesus, His hands, and His feet if we are obedient to the voice of the Spirit.

Every person has a self-will that must be redirected and kept under control. Even work animals have to be "broke" or trained or they are no good as a work animal. Many parents simply do not understand this and think redirecting their child's will somehow will be an injury or injustice to the young child's personality. In my years in the classroom, I used methods of training, always done in love and sympathy, which were good for the children and the society in which we were living. If discipline is not applied early, the youngster grows up to be a spoiled brat, wanting his or her way, throwing temper tantrums, running away, or acting in such a way to bring hurt to the mother and father.

Hard love is the only right way to rear children. During the Depression years, most parents taught their children many valuable lessons, many coming from the Bible. The Book of Proverbs was a very potent and valuable lesson book. Fathers used it in instructing their sons. Most boys raised during my period of growing up learned to respect girls and women. The father would remind us boys when a girl said, "No!" that meant NO.

Also, if a girl wanted to break off a relationship, it was always her decision and right. Lots of men have not been taught this today. It seems lots of women are wising up, getting educations, buying homes, and establishing one-parent homes.

However, there are still lots of good fathers training their children in the right way. Thank God for them. Without effort, boys certainly do not just grow into good, sound, respective husbands and fathers; they must be trained and disciplined, acquainted with hard love and maturity.

Life consists of making decisions and adjusting to change. Seniors are more agitated by change than younger people. We grew up during the mini golden age. Seems funny? This does not refer to science and technology. It means in the nonmaterial aspects of our culture—our churches, schools, our close-knit communities, and what was on our coins was symbolized: *E pluribus Unum*, or "Out of many, one." Loosely translated, "all for one and one for all" was apparent in the attitude of our generation. When disaster came to a member of our community, the whole community pitched in and came to aid in love and sympathy and with our meager worldly possessions. This shows true character and what a person is made of.

This Old House

Our old house, not where I was born but where I lived from ages seven through twenty-three, my formative years, was set on wooden blocks about twenty-two inches from the ground. There were cracks in the floor—we did not need a dust pan as the dirt and debris fell through the cracks as we swept the floor. This kind of house during the Depression was called a cracker house. People in the area where we grew up as well as south of where we lived were jokingly called rednecks, and this land was sometimes called Redneck Riviera.

Being so close to Florida during hurricane season (early fall), often one of these wild and fierce phenomena of nature would rush up to pay us an unhappy visit. In 1925, one of these storms was blowing our way. I was eight years old and sleeping with my father. This old house was rocking and swaying. I was terrified. I felt my heart was right up in my throat. My father said, "Clarence, you are scared, aren't you?"

I said, "Yes, I'm very scared."

He pulled me over next to his body and held me tightly and said, "Clarence, you have no cause to be afraid. I've already talked to the Lord about the storm, and everything is going to be all right. Tomorrow when it is time for us to get out of bed, this old house will still be here."

When Daddy said that, I rolled over on my side of the bed and fell asleep. Sure enough, when I got up the next morning the sun was shining and the old house was still there! Praise the Lord.

When I was ten years old, I planted the trees in back of the house. The tree directly behind the old house is a pecan and was bearing when I was a young boy—and still is.

The kitchen was directly behind the house with a covered catwalk connecting the back porch and house to the kitchen. A large wooden bucket hung there on one side of the catwalk. A wooden-handled dipper also was hung there from a rusty nail. We left the dipper for use by our occasional upper-class sophisticates. They thought we were just dirt farmers—and they were right.

This Old House

This old house has had her stay
Though many years of existing and living
Have brought her many years of decay.

Her doors need squaring—the hinges need oiling
The holes in the chimney need daubing
Cracks in the floor are really appalling.

She has seen families come and seen families go
This disregard of some for upkeep is rated nil
Bad condition year after year grew worse than a pill.

To spruce her up now would bring unhappiness and disdain
Ashes to ashes and dust to dust
Show us people the old lady can trust and entertain.

This old house has endured storms, hurricanes and the like
She survived and stood up ladylike.

The old cracker house of the South
Is outdated and obsolete as the dinosaurs.

Farmer's Almanac

In the spring of the year, all rural children went barefooted. Many parents were pestered every spring: "When can we go barefooted?" The answer given was, "When you see the bumblebees hovering over flowers and hear the whippoorwill calling out in the early part of the night." These were nature's signals that cold weather was gone and early plantings of all kinds of vegetables could begin. This knowledge needs to be preserved because it is a truism and can be beneficial in terms of plantings.

Another truth of nature that should be preserved and thought about concerns the full moon. There are more babies born then than any other day of the month. Nurses know this, especially the older ones. Highway patrol and police tell us more road rage and accidents occur on the full of the moon. They cannot explain it, but they say it definitely does happen.

More farmer's almanac information: Never plow or turn your garden when the ground is so wet that it "slicks up." Soil must crumble when it is ready to plow or cultivate; many gardens and fields are ruined because people don't know much about rural life. We need to learn about our environment. Once I had a neighbor who had a beautiful tree in his backyard. He asked me one year why he never got any pecans from this tree. I told him he never would because it was an ash tree!

Birds and chickens can also be indicators of nature's truisms. Folks raised on a farm know that if the chickens continue to eat when it begins to rain, the rain will continue to fall all day. Having knowledge like this is important, and I am glad I learned it young.

Conditions of Early Life on a Farm

We had one little country store that stayed closed about 75 percent of the time. An old rusty plow hung from one of the rafters of the front porch. A long steel rod hung there to strike the rusty plow when someone came through the door to summon the busy storekeeper who was doing other more important jobs. She finally would come grumbling and complaining about the loose change we each had for candy bars. She knew we weren't going to leave until we spent our money for candy bars. After she would acknowledge us, she would say, "The Sheffield children—and all they want are candy bars. They have been picking strawberries and now that change in their pockets is burning holes in the pockets until they spend it." We didn't understand her symbolic language. All we wanted was candy. She then closed the front door and went back to her house talking to herself. Her husband made a sign and nailed it to the front of the store which read, "No more selling goods on Sunday and damn few through the week." We were learning things that we didn't learn in Sunday school.

We finally grew up and quit banging the old rusty plow to get candy bars. The storekeeper told my father he was glad. He said, "I'm tired of hearing Missouri [his wife] grumble!"

Early Childhood Influences and How They Helped Me Find the Way

Why am I here? What road am I to follow? I asked my parents very early how as a boy I could feel God's hand moving and fitting things in place for the direction my life should take. I ask no one to believe as I do—it is a God-given privilege. I believe every person is destined and given talents even before he or she is conceived in the mother's womb. This does not mean all people will follow the blueprint God has laid out for individuals to follow. He gave each one a choice, a free will, to accept God's plan or to strike out on one's own to make thousands of choices without consulting or asking God, "Why am I here? How will I know the right person to marry? How will I know what God's will is for my life?"

Here is what my parents told me: "Ask your Maker." They told me they asked their Maker and got an answer. "Your Maker is also our Maker," they told me. They taught us children to pray, and God would reveal things to us. Are we teaching our youngsters like this today?

When I was very young, seven or eight years old, a great thing happened to this country boy. I was from the Piney Woods section of south Alabama—freckled-faced, and I wore knee pants and no shoes to church. There was no such thing as saying, "I have decided I will stay home today." We did what Father and Mother told us to do—no mouthing off about anything. They always told us why we should listen and obey: "We love you dearly and would do anything to promote your well being."

Then came the fifth commandment, "honor thy father and mother that thy days shall be long upon the land which the LORD thy God giveth thee." They told us the words in the Bible were God-breathed, and always were true, and everyone could rely on it—thus there was motivation mixed with love that children who honored mother and father were promised a long life.

Then, there was a silence that came over my parents after they asked us our response to what had been said. Here they used the first of the four great principles that motivate all human behavior—recognition, response, new experiences, and desire for security. My parents were fair in their dealings with us children and told us they were not perfect or immortal but were trying their best to bring us up in the nurture and admonition of the Lord.

When a child is in this age of plasticity (very young), he or she is clay in the potter's hand and can be molded into a vessel that will be an enrichment and blessing to all whom he or she comes into contact. When we teach untiringly during this tender age, our children will rise up and call us blessed because God rewards the faithful and obedient parents.

As we continue each day on this pilgrimage of faith journey, we have to pray and ask God to help us because we

Evergreen High School baseball team, 1937.
Clarence is second from left, top row.

are needy creatures and all our feet are made of clay. Some have a string of college degrees, and when dealing with children, education is a good investment and truly helpful. But unless the Holy Spirit is leading, we are only spinning our wheels and getting nowhere. John 15:5 says "without me ye can do nothing." The ground is level at the foot of the cross. Without the shed blood of our Lord there is no remission of sin.

My parents were not educated but they were godly parents who held family devotions. With a worn Bible and sitting in a big rocking chair with a bottom made of white oak splits, Papa would read as the four boys and four girls would stand as close to him as we could. In many respects we were as poor as church mice, but we were all loved and each respected.

During my early teens, my younger brother Wesley led me to practice baseball every free minute we had. He was a southpaw and never threw a straight ball. When he was not pitching, he played shortstop. The first baseman knew him and was always ready for the curve ball to first base. I played third base and was near the crowd at the ballpark. The spectators helped me greatly—they would rag me terribly, and it helped me conquer my shyness. I discovered our coach really had an interest in me and was a warm, enthusiastic person who seemed never too busy to offer a boy much-needed encouragement and hope. He taught me how to stand a little behind the plate and step into the pitched ball.

The coach became my idol, and I respected him very much. He was a hero figure in my early life, and this was leading up to my surrendering to Jesus Christ.

Here is where my spiritual journey really began. The old church building had wires crisscrossing inside the building and separating the classes. Many teenagers liked the way the classrooms were divided by curtain partitions. If some students became bored, they would just listen to the teacher on the other side of the curtain.

Here I had a teacher—the human being I considered the most like Jesus. His name was Uncle Bill Smith. With God's help, this man wrote on each boy's heart and mind with an indelible spiritual pencil never to be erased. Such love and compassion and humility we had never experienced.

Our central theme for the quarter was the biblical principle of going the extra mile. My father told me a story about Uncle Bill that showed that my teacher practiced what he preached.

In those days, nearly every family had a piece of land they carved out of the woods with ax, crosscut saw, and mallet by hard work and much blood, sweat, and tears. This was called new ground.

The brush was burned in huge piles when it was dry. There were many stumps to deal with. Every plow had a cutting coulter fastened to its beam to cut the little roots before the plow got to this point.

Uncle Bill was plowing in his new ground. His horse's name was Molly, and as soon as the plow struck even a small root, Ole Molly would stop—whereupon Uncle Bill would lift the plow and cluck to Ole Molly to get her to go. Uncle Bill would hold the plow up and wait for Molly to start up again. She would finally start, and then the man and his horse would begin the same process all over again.

Uncle Bill would have that angelic look on his face as he talked to Ole Molly while holding the plow and waiting for her to start again. He would say, "Molly, you and I are a team, and with the Lord's help, we just got to get this plowing done!"

Ole Molly would turn her head back or sideways and look at Uncle Bill as if she were in complete agreement and knew exactly what Uncle Bill was saying. He always kept his smile and did not fret.

My father said, "Uncle Bill is a godly man and loves everybody." At church, there was a large chair that was placed up front right under the podium. This was Uncle Bill's seat. The preacher could have reached down and touched him on his head if he had wanted to. His angelic look toward the audience did wonders, and put us all in a spirit of worship. His prayers touched heaven.

With Uncle Bill as our teacher, we were like clay in the potter's hand. Every Sunday we were asked to share what we did the week before to show we wanted to go that extra mile for Jesus. We were told what to expect ahead of time, so we could tell our beloved teacher what we did. God was at work using this man to write on our young impressionable hearts and minds.

I was a young, shy lad, but Uncle Bill taught us all to pray. I did not know exactly how to go that extra mile, but God told me when I asked Him. Here is what I was led to do. My job on the farm was to draw water from a well and pour it in a large trough—usually fourteen pails, so I drew sixteen pails (buckets we called them). Usually I also gave a pad of peanut hay to the animals, filled with nuts which did not get threshed out. The mules really relished this hay, so I gave each animal an extra pad filled with peanuts. This was going the extra mile for me.

The next week in Sunday school when my turn came, I told what message I got, who gave it to me, and what I did. I thought Uncle Bill was just going on to heaven then. This kind of teaching was inspirational. This biblical principle helped change my whole life. How we should stand in awe of God!

When I returned from World War II in the Pacific, I went back to the Old Camp Ground Church at Mt. Union and stood there looking at the headstone on Uncle Bill's grave. Somehow I had the warmest feeling—indulge me a little here—that God might have a peep hole in heaven and took Uncle Bill by the hand and led him over so he could look down and see me. I felt I was indeed standing on holy ground.

So for me, Uncle Bill will never die. He is basking on the flower-bedecked banks of the sweet forever. By God's grace I will meet Uncle Bill by-and-by. He is living on in the hearts and lives of those he loved and taught.

This great man of faith put an indelible stamp on those he taught. As we know, this stamping cannot be erased—it is permanent. That is why it is so necessary and important to teach without ceasing while the child is in his or her formative years. Uncle Bill taught that life is a series of making choices. The choices we make have consequences. When we do what is wrong, we have to pay. Paying can happen in many ways.

We all at birth are self-willed, and this will has to be redirected or broken. Do not get disturbed now. I am not talking about breaking the spirit. Redirecting the self-will must be done in love. Teaching must prevail here, or great harm can be done.

Shirley, Wayne, and Clarence in 1949.

I will give a true-life example here for clarification. When our daughter, Shirley, was three years of age she had a little doll; for some unknown reason she threw the doll down on the floor and stomped it. Her mother told her to pick the doll up. Her little face reddened, and she said, "I'll not do it." Mother explained that she was her mother and loved her very much and hated to cause her pain, but if she did not pick up the doll, she must be punished. Mother had to punish Shirley—three spankings before she would obey and pick up the little doll.

From that day forward Shirley has always been obedient and loving to both of us. When a child is placed in our arms to love, train, and enjoy, there is an equal responsibility to nurture, teach, love and direct the child as best we can under the guidance of God. This is fundamental.

Later in our lives, we lived with Shirley in her big house near Nashville, Tennessee. We could never hope to be near anyone more compassionate, unselfish, and diligently working every day to make Mother and Dad comfortable and happy. To do this for two retired senior citizens was no easy task, but our daughter loves us as we love her.

First Grade Teacher

My first teacher was one of the world's greatest—she had a unique way of being pleasant and optimistic. When it came time to be stern with no foolishness, she could communicate that perfectly. She was a redheaded, unmarried woman, and my parents called her an old maid. I didn't know what that meant.

She made learning fun. My love of reading goes back to her clever way of challenging us children. She taught and loved us as *individuals*, not as a class. She used *recognition* when we would come through for her. Her sternness and her love for every child challenged me at that early age of seven.

In my early work in elementary education as a principal, I learned that nobody on the staff had as much influence on the minds of young children as the first grade teacher. Many are numbered among the "great."

Later, romance evidently came to this redheaded first grade teacher. So, afterwards my parents could not call her an old maid, but Mrs. Harper. I was glad.

What Teenage Boys Did for Recreation

Necessity is the mother of invention. All teenage youngsters want to do something they call recreation. In my time, ages twelve to twenty (1929–1937), we invented some things to do. Remember these were Depression years, and money was hard to get. Nearly all people where we lived were farmers. We cleared lots of land—cut the trees, sawed it into lumber, and cut the underbrush and branches (limbs to us). Some was cut into firewood to be used in the fireplaces and cookstoves.

Boys would gather at one of these piles of branches, bushes, and straw. A big fire was built, and we brought things we would eat and drink. This was to be a bird thrashing. Each boy had splinters lighted on one end. Now, we were ready to rush to the nearest pile of brush, surrounding it quickly. On each side one's foot would shake the brush pile, and birds would come out fluttering, trying to get away as the swatting began.

Seldom would a bird get away. One person would gather up our dinner and carry it to the fire and start pulling off the feathers. This was continued until each brush pile had been thrashed.

Sometimes during the thrashing, a mistake was made and one of us got a good swatting. This was fun, and we had a good laugh about it.

We carried home brew we had made ourselves, capping it when the blue smoke started swirling out. It was left in a cool spring already capped and ready for the next outing. We invented a game called Hitting the Peg. We built outdoor basketball courts and used the iron rim from a whiskey barrel for our goals. We also played touch football. Baseball was played lots during these hard times of the Depression.

My High School Days, 1934–1938

My high school days began in the ninth grade at Evergreen High School in 1934. I had a poor self-image, but I loved sports—played varsity football from 1935 to 1937. My position was right end, number eleven. We played offense as well as defense due to the shortage of players. Our right tackle taught me everything I knew, not the coach. Our left end was larger than I was, a better tackler and a better blocker, but he simply could not catch a football. This is what I did best. That was the specialty that put me on the team. In 1937, three players on this team won scholarships to play at two Mississippi colleges—our left tackle, center, and right end. The left tackle and center went to Ole Miss; my scholarship was to Milsaps in Jackson, Mississippi. My parents talked me out of playing football in college—they kindly bribed me. I fell for this, and I'm glad I did.

In high school I had algebra under my coach, and I failed it as flat as a pancake. Then there was an inspirational teacher who had a little session with this fellow who thought

Evergreen High School. Clarence is third from left, back row.

he could not learn algebra. She told me she was going to teach algebra next semester, and that I was going to be in her class. She also told me I had lots of potential and drive.

Being a teenager I laughed at her. She was a little lady, unmarried, but God must have destined her for teaching. She was the greatest teacher I ever had. She, like myself, had never won a beauty contest, but honestly she had a heart as big as a boxcar.

Yes, I took algebra under Miss Moore and made an A. In all her classes she used the first principle that motivates all human behavior—recognition. I was beginning to believe I could learn lots of things. She recognized me as a person who felt inferior, and she worked on it.

I took physics, chemistry, and biology with Miss Moore also and did well in all of these subjects. The English language does not have enough adjectives to describe this inspirational teacher. One day she told me, "Clarence, you might be a teacher right here in this county one day." I knew it was not time for "mights." I was young and foolish, and again I laughed at what she said. Ignorance is a terrible thing—and I had plenty of it. If I could have bottled it, I could have "ignorized" the whole county because sure enough, in the fall of 1940, I was a teacher of grade six at Annex School in Conecuh County!

Words! Words! Many times our words and the words of others sustain us and lift us up when we are in the valley of despondency. Miss Moore would say, "Don't recross bridges, keep going—don't look back." This dear lady had spiritual discernment. She had spiritual twenty-twenty vision.

I thought of Isaiah 40:30 many times on the battlefield as I pillowed my head on a metal .30-caliber machine gun ammunition box trying to sleep. I would look into the heavens and pray and claim every promise in Psalm 91. There Miss Moore's words would come to me loud and clear, "Clarence, you have special qualities."

When I heard all this at Evergreen High, I didn't believe it. I was like an ant crawling on a ball—I couldn't see very far. When I lay in the battlefield, I wondered if I ever would again lie down on a clean bed and trade this ammo box for a soft pillow. God blessed me and answered my prayers. There is no country on earth like America.

Now as I am an old man, I reminisce and remember the words of Miss Moore—they bless my life and lift me up—for a time I soar in heavenly places. The other day I found a memory book I had bought back in 1934. Many friends had written in it for me all through the 1930s. The humor and composition styles have changed over the years, but in reading it again, I find young people back then were very much as they are today. Sometimes, we need to be taken back in nostalgia to former years.

Teenage Runaway

As a teenage boy, I always loved sports and liked to excel. Our right tackle, Tom, was a large man and hard as nails. I will admit he played what I called dirty football. He taught me everything I knew. I always talked to him and tried to get him to see that if a man could not do it fair and square, it was cowardly to resort to dirty tactics. He would just laugh and say nothing. One evening we played a team up in Butler County, Alabama, and he got what was coming to him. Two guys ganged up on Tom. The doctors told our coach every rib on his left side was broken. He was out for a long time. When he started playing again, he quit that dirty stuff.

My parents never wanted me to play football, but being all wise and incorrigible in some of my ways, I played anyway. One night as we were playing Andalusia, Alabama, our chief rival, I tackled one of their largest players. He twisted around while going down and fell on my neck. I had wryneck and could hardly move at all. My family gave me such a hard time, I went to my sister's who lived in Walnut Hill, Florida, twelve miles south of Atmore, Alabama.

There I got a job crating Satsuma oranges in a large crating shed at Walnut Hill. One week, and I thought that was enough for me. Then, I was furnished a long, light ladder and started picking pinecones for the mast. Nurseries used these seeds to get thousands of pine seedlings. They sold them to paper wood companies to plant in rows over much of their land. Pine burs have stickers on the outside. I had no gloves, and after one week my hands were bloody and sore.

I started to think. I was like the prodigal son in some ways. I realized I had it good at home; so I went home, went back to school, and the next thing I knew, I was playing football again.

Once I overheard my parents talking—they didn't know I was listening. In a situation like that, one's hearing improves. My father said, "We got to get Clarence into something other than farming or logging. He marches to a different drummer than the rest of our boys."

I wanted to say, "Amen," but I didn't think it wise to do that, so I said it to myself silently. As you'll see later, after I finished high school, a door did swing open during the height of the Depression, and I jumped at the opportunity. It was really tough then, but I kept working, studying, and praying.

I guess there's nothing that opens our eyes like being enrolled in the School of Hard Knocks. Adversity seems to introduce a man to himself. I really learned my lesson, and it changed my attitude toward my family members. Their prayers were answered. After this, the fifth commandment really came alive, and I have told my children this story. It is a promise. They are so loving and caring for Dad (and Mother before she died) now. I am so happy and well cared for. Praise the Lord!

Fishermen's Lives on South Palafox Street

In early 1941 my father and mother moved to Pensacola, Florida, since he could no longer operate the farm without the help of his two younger sons who were in the service. Dad worked in a defense plant there until the war was over.

He then owned and operated a restaurant on South Palafox Street, as far south as one can go without entering the water of the Gulf of Mexico. Ninety-five percent of his customers were fishermen. They would go out on one boat; each man knew what his job was and did it. They knew the kind of fish they wanted and where they would likely be. There was no set time to return—sometimes it was a week, sometimes two. Weather permitting, they would stay sometimes much longer until their reefers were filled, then they would come in.

I was amazed at the camaraderie of these fellows. They would stay right there on South Palafox until all the money was gone. When one had a dollar, the other had money. When all were flat broke, they would go back to sea. Wine, women, and song seemed to be all that mattered to these fellows.

My father kept a cigar box under a counter to keep a record of all financial transactions. Sometimes when a slightly drunk fisherman would finish eating he would give my dad a wad of bills, and it was no use to argue with one in that state. Dad knew them by name, so he would count the money and note the date he received it, along with the price of the food. The next day when this one was sober and eating again, my dad would take the price of his meal and return the rest of his money to him.

Sometimes one of this number would have too much to drink while eating and would fall face down in his plate. His buddies would drag him back and wash him up and put him to bed. Next day he was sober. It seemed to be a cycle.

They all loved my father, calling him Dad. When my father died, the ship must have been in because here was this bunch of comrades standing around the casket, bearded, many unwashed, but tears trickling down extremely tanned skin. Their refrain, one and all, was: "Dad has crossed over . . . He was a good man. We gonna miss him *so* much!"

As my father was lowered into Mother Earth there in the Pensacola Heights cemetery after the "ashes to ashes and dust to dust" phrase was uttered, I walked away with these words in my heart and mind: "Lord, help me to love and to have compassion like my dad." I needed help to acquire the above traits. Humanity with all its inducements and temptations would never allow me to come up with what Dad had without *that* higher power to help me.

"Where There's a Will, There's a Way:"

High School Graduation and Daphne State Normal, 1938–1940

As our graduation date was approaching on May 28, 1938, the war clouds were gathering as Hitler had already gobbled up two little countries and was threatening to invade all the low countries. The situation really looked gloomy.

America knew this madman had to be stopped. We weren't at war, but most people could see the handwriting on the wall far in advance. The country was in a terrible state of being unprepared, but our high school principal told us to beware and be ready. "We are counting on you boys and girls to join up to meet the challenge!" We did—95 percent of my classmates, male and female, eventually "joined up."

We were in the height of the Depression. Money was almost as scarce as hen's teeth. My principal informed me I could go to Daphne State Normal, and I could work on the campus—painting, plastering, planting grass, raking leaves, and doing anything else that needed to be done. He told me the government checks would only pay my tuition and books. I didn't know where the rest was coming from. I prayed and decided to step out on faith. I had enough money for a bus ride to Daphne, Alabama, on Mobile Bay.

When I arrived, I had only some change in my pocket—that was all. I was the last person to register. I was sitting in a hall that connected the president's office and the library. The president's wife was the librarian. She walked into her husband's office and said, "What are we going to do with this one?"

He said, "We are taking him home with us." He drove a 1938 Oldsmobile. I got loaded up, and we drove one mile up to an old colonial home that was picturesque and enchanting with a large veranda across the entire front of the building. From the house, the terrain sloped downward to the edge of the water of Mobile Bay facing westward.

That night we ate a light meal, and I was introduced to the president's mother-in-law, who was active in the Catholic church and came to serve as my unofficial godmother. She greeted me very graciously and then escorted me to the second floor with three bay windows.

Mine was the middle bay window. The room had one small bed and a little table. From the ceiling there hung a cord and a twenty-five-watt bulb that was turned on by the small cord. She told me, "This is your room," and then she left. There was dust on the little table, and almost everything seemed to be covered with it. It looked as if it were about an eighth of an inch thick. I hope I am not exaggerating.

I had never felt so uncertain and homesick in my life and prayed, "Lord if you let me live until tomorrow, I intend to hitchhike back to Evergreen, my home."

It was a foggy night, and the ships coming up from the Gulf of Mexico had to follow buoys with lights on the tops to mark the channel. The channel was dredged regularly so no ship would run aground. All night these ships coming up to enter Mobile Bay had the worst, woeful sound! This was adding insult to injury, and I couldn't sleep. When morning finally came, I knew some people had been praying for me, and this caused me to change my mind. I stayed, went to work, and cleaned the place.

I attended Mass when they did; we always went to the Catholic church. The godmother talked to me lots and told me she was praying for me, and I know she was. I needed somebody to help me pray, and this godmother did that for me, and I dearly loved her.

Every evening after my last class, I walked through the wooded area to the old colonial home with the bay windows. Mrs. Alexander sat in her favorite rocker on the veranda, quoting her favorite Scripture, Psalm 19. As the sun was sinking in the west, what a marvelous picture it made! "The Heavens declare the glory of God and the firmament showeth his handiwork. Day unto day uttereth speech and night unto night showeth knowledge. There is no speech nor language where their voice is not heard" (Ps. 19:1–3). I lived with these dear people my freshman year, and they helped impact my life.

My sophomore year I moved into an apartment that was run down and unsightly. I was rooming with a boy from Mobile, Alabama. We worked together on the campus doing anything that needed done. Once he said, "Clarence, you are always singing as we work—where did you learn these songs?"

I replied, "I learned them in Sunday school."

He was not reared in a Christian home, but he was listening and thinking. Those were tough days for me, but daily I told myself that every day brought me closer to graduation, and the Lord was helping me.

Beginning My College Days:

Temptations Galore While Wrestling with Poverty

Social life in 1938–1940 was very different from what it is today. The folkways and mores of that time are practically opposite the present social framework.

My freshman year I honestly didn't have too many dates—it mostly consisted of groups of young girls and boys walking out to the ends of long piers that extended out into Mobile Bay. There at the end of the pier was a restroom of sorts. There were tables set up there—never found out why. We reasoned the shrimpers ate there.

The gender ratio was 10:1, ten girls to every boy. The first year while I lived with the president, I was rather aloof and shy as I knew I was being watched closely. All social activities had to happen on Friday afternoon or evening because we weren't there to find a mate, although some did. As I said before, the war clouds were gathering, and some girls left school and returned to their hometowns to get their man before Uncle Sam did—they made these confessions.

One day the biology teacher was late to our class, but some smart aleck got there first and wrote these words on the board, "Those here who are working on a 'Mrs.' degree meet at the mail room door immediately after this class." Funny, eight or ten girls flocked to see if they had mail from home!

The rigid rule of no dating unless it was on Friday afternoon or evening made the difference between academic success and failure. Freshman year is a crucial year for anyone who really means business.

My sophomore year I was in a different situation, but we still didn't go out every night—only on Friday night. Certain girls who had cars in Daphne knew when to appear where we lived—in a rather secluded place near the beach. They would come up and scratch with a coin or nail on the screen, and that was the signal for us to come out. We all would load up and drive twenty-one miles south to Fairhope, Alabama, to the American Legion Hall. Music was played until midnight every Friday night, and mostly somebody else fed the jukebox, so this met our fancy. I never danced so much in my life! The record, *South of the Border Down Mexico Way*, was played so much it was worn out.

Here at Daphne Normal the boys were the chased; the girls were the chasers. From watching TV today, it seems this form of socializing and attracting a mate has not changed much.

Two months before I graduated from Daphne State, I was rooming with a fellow who went home one Friday afternoon to Mobile, Alabama. Our room was upstairs in a very large house. The owner of the house was Mrs. Harris, a widow. She was away for some reason this weekend.

There was a family that lived a very short distance from the Harris home. They had two daughters. One was married and lived one block from the college. The other girl was in her late teens—this is my guess. Actually, I'm not sure about her age, but she was a beauty and appeared to weigh about 118 pounds. She had jet-black hair and looked like a model.

As you can see, I had to include this part; it is part of the true story of my journey of life. Every word is true and I was reluctant to include it, but it is part of my past.

About 1:15 P.M. on this Sunday, I heard footsteps coming up the stairs from the lower floor. My door was partially ajar. Her family was on vacation, she said, and they lived about a quarter of a mile from where I was rooming. I had seen her several times as she walked to where her sister lived, but I never acted in any way like I was interested in a date with her.

Her feelings towards me were apparently different. She walked right through my doorway and stuck out her hand. Naturally, I would not refuse to shake hands with a beauty appearing so unexpectedly—I was shocked really. She pulled on my hand and started backing out the door. She said, "I want you to come and walk with me in the romantic glades."

What could I say! So, I complied, and we walked past her home until we finally got to the spot she had mentioned. She was right; it was a secluded romantic spot.

It was warm that evening and there was lots of straw on the ground everywhere. She sat down and gave my hand a tug as a signal to sit down, too, and I did. Honest confession—I guess I grew up in a sheltered environment, but at this time I was a virgin—if that word applies to a male. I was chaste I guess is the word.

Immediately I thought of what my father taught us boys in the sixth chapter of Proverbs. It was very strong then and still is. I was filled with fear because I didn't know what her true motive was in all her antics and aggressive behavior since I was really a stranger to her.

She told me about all her fantasies and her desire for tall men. She pulled her skirt halfway up on her thighs and lay flat on her back with her hands joined behind her head. I didn't know if she was pregnant and was trying to rope me into marriage, since she knew I was to graduate soon or just what to make of it.

She was so brazen. But listen now—the truth again—I was completely impotent for the time being, and I did not lie with her. It was the only time in my life that I was like that until I was eighty-two years old.

I was very much afraid and in a stage of confusion. This may account for my impotence, or it could have been that my mother and father were praying for their son. I don't know what happened, but I'm glad it happened the way it did—guess she thought I was a freak, but that was all right.

About one month later this girl was married. I never saw her again. I always wondered about this girl. How did she know my roommate was away that weekend? Also, how did she know Mrs. Harris was away? I still believe the Almighty's hand was there, taking care of this innocent and inexperienced country boy.

Right across the street from the college lived the Wallace family. Two college girls roomed with them, and my roommate and I used to go there at times and dance until all hours. The Wallaces were dear friends of ours, and they knew we were lonely. These were our last months at dear, old Daphne State. Our class was the last (1940). The college was closed and all records sent to Livingston State in Livingston, Alabama.

Now there is a large Catholic school located where the Daphne State Normal used to be. On the grounds a large hotel stands. It was built before the Civil War. During Farragut's Battle of Mobile Bay, a cannonball hit this hotel to the right of the front entrance on the lower floor of the veranda. The hole is big enough to poke a large coconut through. Today, it is still not patched or repaired. It was left so people would know Admiral Farragut had been there! It is part of history as well as part of this Catholic school.

I thank all my Catholic and Protestant friends of Daphne who helped me, tutored me, and prayed for me in my trials and foolish years of growing up. I survived being a teenager. I really came of age in 1940 because I was thrust into life head over heels and had to figure it all out. With God holding my hand and my dear mother and father praying, how could I not succeed?

Daphne:

Tribulation to Success

Honestly speaking, those two years at Daphne State Normal tried my faith and resolve more than I could ever put in words: poverty, temptations, depending on things I could not see, disequilibrium from not knowing the outcome of my grades, hunger, lack of wardrobe and personal necessities, and other things of this nature. I gained an important principle of learning—the fear of the Lord is the beginning of knowledge.

One cold gray day I was trying to hitchhike my way home, which was one hundred miles to the north. I was hungry, had no money, and needed lots of help. This was my second year at Daphne. I was wearing a green sweater with a large white "E" on it that I won in football. Before that day, I had gone anywhere I had wanted to go—people would pick me up as soon as they saw this sweater.

I stood on the corner of Main Street and old 31 Highway, and people ignored me this morning. I stood there quite a while, and it began raining lightly. I was at my point of desperation, and I bowed my head and sent an SOS to the Lord. I said, "Lord, when I accepted you as Savior, I trusted you, and you promised never to leave me nor forsake me. I need you desperately."

I raised my head and looked directly across the street at a home. The door opened and a lady came out. She looked so different from most people—she had a glow about her head and face, and she came straight to me with questions. I told her my problems, and she invited me into her home. She got a hot drink and some sandwiches and introduced me to her husband who was shaving. She said, "My husband is in the paper wood business and is going to Greenville, Alabama, in about thirty minutes. You may ride with him as he travels up old 31 Highway—going right through your hometown, Evergreen."

I can tell you I was on cloud nine. I had heard about miracles and angels before, and after that day, I knew they were real. I have told this many times and in many different places. The Lord was using me in this college, and at the time I didn't even know it. I know it now. My roommate was saved, and he was from a non-Christian home. God works in mysterious ways.

One evening my roommate and I had nothing to eat. Our apartment had a fence around it. The gate was open and a large, fat hen came in the yard and went into a small enclosure, and we closed it. We decided to kill the hen. I cooked it, and we had chicken for two days. It was not Kentucky Fried Chicken, but it was good to two hungry students. I never felt guilty about it because I believed it was divine providence.

Then we got a large supply of food from home. God took care of our needs until we graduated in May 1940. "The Wonder of It All" is a song that rings a spiritual bell when I hear it. My cup runneth over!

Anxious Days:

Summer 1940

I had just graduated from Daphne State in May and had a two-year diploma that certified me to teach. I was hired as a teacher the first week I was home and started teaching in my first school, the sixth grade at Annex School in Conecuh County where I was reared.

After two and a half months, my principal came to me and asked if I were in the National Guard. I told him I was. Mobilization was November 25, 1940. He suggested that I get married, and I would not have to go. He seemed to think I should, but I was not serious or in love.

That evening I went out into a field of crotalaria (legume for soil enrichment). It was about waist deep, and it was sowed broadcast. It was yellow as gold and so beautiful! I knelt down in this field and sent another SOS to God. I told Him what my principal had suggested (like He didn't know). I didn't think that would be the right thing to do, although it would pain me to leave my first teaching job.

I didn't intend to leave the field until I got an answer. I got an answer right back—go on to the year of training you are called out to do. I was so relieved. Because of the growing problems in the world, I had this gnawing feeling that I might have to leave if I took this job. I don't think the superintendent of education knew what we National Guardsmen knew or he would not have hired me. I felt guilty for not leveling with him.

Before I received my answer from God, I did much pondering about the loophole to avoid the war if I were married. Every teenage boy at a certain age fantasizes about what kind of girl he wants to marry. I thought, "Now, maybe there is an escape route here for me." I had seen a girl in Daphne a few months earlier who was my ideal in size, measurements, height, hair, and eyes—yes, *everything*, except she was too aggressive and a chaser. I knew if I could find another like her, excluding her aggressive behavior, I might fall in love and get married, and then I would not have to leave my first school.

I was in my hometown a few days later, and I saw a girl working in the Rex Theater that I thought was an exact replica of this other girl in Daphne. I did not know whether she was married. I looked and saw no rings, but I had no one to introduce me to her and didn't know what kind of approach to make.

Another quandary! Poor boy! I walked over to her and said, "Hello, Beautiful! I was staring at you for obvious reasons, and I apologize for my rudeness." We left there together, and she was a beauty for sure, but she was not a conversationalist. She showed no interest at all in her conquest. I thought, "Well, I guess I should have left her at the theater." I thought maybe she had had a bad day at the theater. I tried every technique in the book but to no avail. I decided I'd give her one more chance, and I did. It was a wet blanket affair.

I decided, "Well, I will have to go on to Camp Blanding, Florida, and put in my year of National Guard training." I knew that I was not going to marry at that time because I was not in love. To marry without love would be the tragedy of tragedies. I prayed about it a great deal.

Part 2

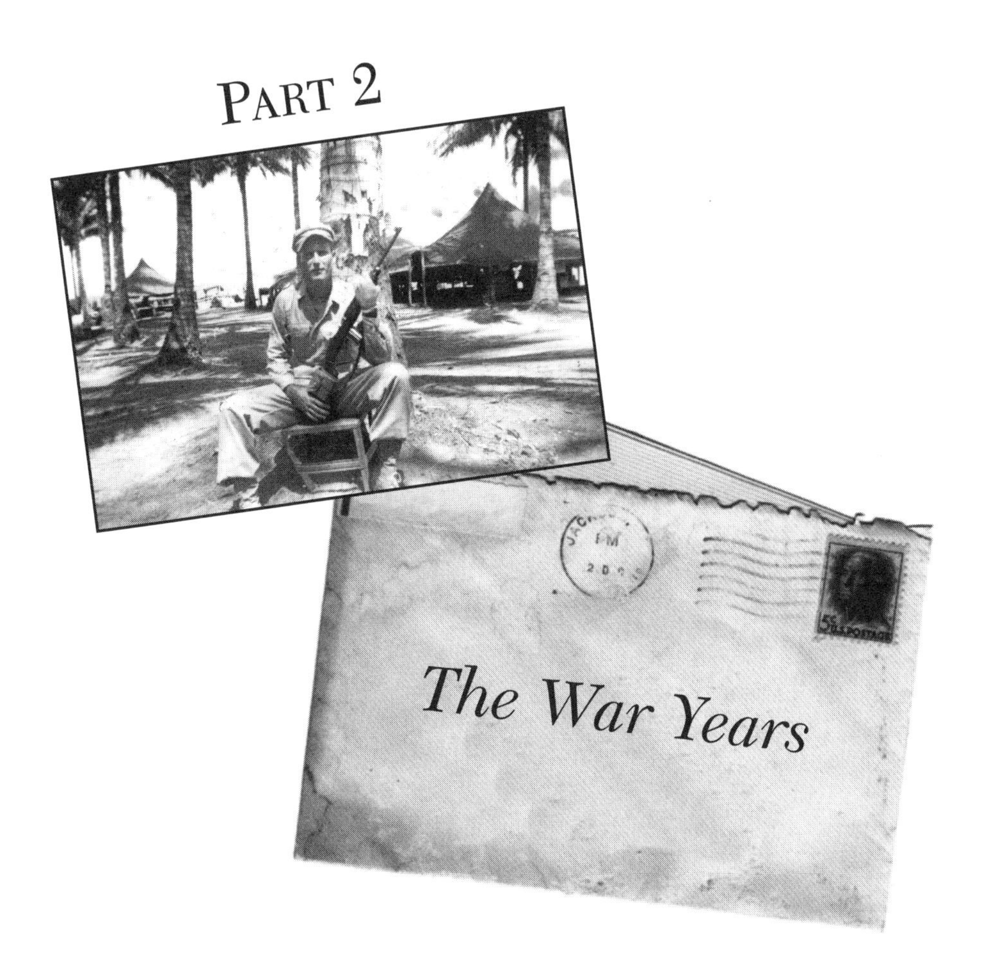

The War Years

You're in the Army Now!

My military unit Battery C 117 Field Artillery left Evergreen, Alabama, on January 1, 1941, for Camp Blanding, Florida. Guess it might be stretching the truth a little by calling it a camp. The latrines were usable but far from completion. Our mess halls were completed, and that was it. All one could see were sand dunes and turkey scrub oaks. The camp was located on the edge of Kingsley Lake—aerial photographs show it as round as a silver dollar. All water for Camp Blanding came from Kingsley Lake near Starke, Florida. When I left my first school in 1940 to train at Camp Blanding, there were thirteen sets of brothers in our Battery C. I understand this was true in almost all guard units called out prior to our involvement in World War II. My brother Wesley was in Battery C also.

When the USS *Juneau*, a light cruiser near Guadalcanal, was sunk in 1942, five brothers were lost. What a blow to a family in Waterloo, Iowa! This news reached many people in the armed services and many people in the United States.

Many were shocked that all these brothers were assigned to the same ship. This caused the commander in chief and his cabinet to split up these guard units (if they could), which came from little hometowns. This was wise because if a company or battery was completely wiped out in a battle, and they all were from the same small town, the morale of the people in that town would be devestated. This was wisdom and just another reason I love America.

Some units were not split up. I have reason to believe there were good reasons why they weren't—perhaps they were already overseas. While growing up as a country boy, I never dreamed or had the faintest idea where I would go, what I would be called on to do, and the multitudinous choices I would have to make while I lived. Without a supreme, divine Guide I would have been like a ship at sea without a rudder, tossed aimlessly about.

We were soldiers and builders at Camp Blanding our first few months. We followed our schedule to the letter—I was in survey and fire control. After two months of study and using the method of "aiming circle laying of battery" for firing of four 105 Howitzers, three of us were eligible for a corporal rating.

The battery commander and the executive officer could not decide who should get the rating. They finally decided to give each of us a speed test to see which one could lay the battery the fastest for firing. I laid the battery for firing the fastest, so I got a corporal rating. Buck privates got a dollar a day, and my pay jumped to fifty-six dollars a month. I thought I was wealthy.

Then, I bought my first car, a secondhand 1938 Ford four-door black De Luxe. In June 1941, I was asked to become the mess sergeant if I would take the job. Our mess sergeant had physical problems and had to be relieved. I accepted and was made a staff sergeant. This was a regular and important job. I enjoyed it very much. I had some of the best cooks in the battalion and some who couldn't boil water—an exaggeration, of course, but they had to be supervised and watched closely. Every soldier was from south Alabama at first. We all understood one another. We all spoke the same language.

Four of us soldiers got a weekend pass to go home to Evergreen, Alabama. We were out all night on Saturday night and came in Sunday morning as it was getting light December 7. We heard the tragic news of Pearl Harbor and were told to return to camp immediately. We did.

I will back up here a little. November 25, 1941, completed our year, and our president decided to extend our time six more months. We all knew what was on the horizon and why. That year at Camp Blanding we had practically nothing to fight with. In playing war games and assimilating certain conditions, we even laid one sapling across another as our antitank gun at a crossroad.

We had so little and realized our families and loved ones could be in jeopardy because of a lack of military weapons. We had one Bar Browning automatic rifle in our battery and a few '03 rifles, which were obsolete and practically worthless.

There is no wonder that we did not walk out the gates when our year of training was up. We had hope as we prayed that somehow our people would become aroused to action, and they did. America astounded the world with how quickly we got every kind of new weapon and ammunition we needed. The good people on the home front will never be forgotten because they worked and sacrificed and supported us so well.

From the sand dunes and turkey oaks of Camp Blanding, Florida, came many stories and romantic episodes during the most explosive time of my life—guess the "urge to merge" was strengthened by the uncertainty and war clouds hanging low over us continually. Such situations cause young men to think, "Here I am today, and beyond there is no certainty, so I better explore and find some meaning to 'all this' before I just lie there under a white cross and take up a little space for eternity—never experiencing *love* and *life* as the Almighty intended it."

In my eighty-seven years, I have seen thousands of examples of the earmarks of war on society caused by damming up the creative urges and desires by herding men up and moving them off for long periods of time to fight in seemingly never-ending wars. This seems to me to be wrong and detrimental to a civilized society.

In 1941, we would take trips, lots of them, riding on GI trucks—two seats, one on each side of the truck. Traffic was rather sparse then compared to now, and the weather was warm so the canvas cover was rolled up and tied so everybody could see the beautiful lakes, orange groves, beaches, and yes, the girls who would line the edge of the street to wave and cheer. These girls would write their addresses, telephone numbers, etc., on a piece of paper, fasten it with a rubber band to a small stick of wood the size of a little finger, and throw it to the men in the truck.

As the trucks would roll slowly through the towns, a girl could almost look the crew over and hand-deliver her mail without a stamp, avoiding pitching it into the bed of the GI truck and causing a scramble. We were rolling through Deland, a city in Volusa County, Florida, where there was a certain college, and that day I received one of these letters.

On a weekend after we were back, I decided to call the girl whose address was on that small piece of paper. She was so excited, and so was this soldier! She lived in Jacksonville on Winter Street. Her name was Edith.

Jacksonville, the first largest city from Camp Blanding, wasn't far for a lonely soldier looking for a date. Edith impressed me very much just talking over the phone. She was a nineteen-year-old brunette with a dark complexion. She was a good conversationalist, extreme optimist, and knew when to talk and when to listen. I almost fell in love with her on my first date, but it is never wise to let too much out on the first few dates.

Time rolled on and I knew we were getting serious but uncertainty and the war held me back—I knew it was a matter of months if not weeks before we'd be in war up to our eye sockets.

Sure enough, we were deeply in love—then Pearl Harbor. We were engaged and all of a sudden, we soldiers found ourselves deep in the heart of Texas at Camp Bowie. Then it was cactus, mesquite, and squeaking oil pumping—Squeak! Squeak! All the time. Our nearest town was Brownwood—if a pin were stuck in Brownwood, it would be in the center of Texas.

It hurts to be put in a situation like this. I finally laid the true facts before her and told her not to wait on me. She knew I loved her, and I knew she loved me; but there's nothing so foolish as to wait, and wait, and waste away. If by chance I did not come back, two lives would be lost to love and life.

After much soul-searching and suffering, Edith agreed. Later she was married to a navy man. I thought, "Well, it is a victory for the navy, but what about the army?" At that time, I could not say it was a victory for the army because I knew I had to overcome my feelings of loss.

What did I learn from this painful experience? "Keep your hand in the Hand that stills the waters; keep your hand in the Hand that stills the seas." Later, the Lord led me to "Miss Right." He knows better than we know. In humanity, we are looking through a glass darkly. If this had not happened I would not have married my wonderful wife, Reitha, and had two fine children, Shirley Ann and Wayne. Many of my fellow comrades could not withstand such experiences as I have stated and not succumb to drugs, liquor, sex, gambling, and lost family life.

After two months in Texas we were sent to Louisiana maneuvers. After this we were sent to Camp Shelby, Mississippi. Here, our division was split up. In each company, or battery, a skeleton company was kept, a first sergeant, four Howitzer sergeants, a mess sergeant, a supply sergeant, a communication sergeant, and a survey sergeant. Then our whole new division launched into training draftees. This training took place at Camp Shelby.

It was here that an officer came to me and said he had checked my record; because I had attended two years of college, he felt I could make it in Officer Candidate School (OCS). After I thought about it, I decided that since I had some training in fire control I could make it. So, I filled out the necessary papers and handed them to my commanding officer.

Next, the order came for me to report to Ft. Benning, Georgia. I figured it was a mistake, but finally I found out they were sending me to an infantry OCS to become a second lieutenant in the infantry. I originally thought that since most of my training was in the National Guard—sixteen months at

Blanding and Camp Bowie and also some at Ft. Sill where the guys went to become second lieutenants in field artillery—I would be sent to Ft. Sill, Oklahoma. However, that was not the case.

At Ft. Benning, I slept between two genuine fellows. One from Fresno, California, and the other was a bachelor who had been teaching sociology and economics at Holy Cross before entering the army to serve his country. We read the Scripture and prayed before taps. His last name began with "Sh" like mine. This was why we were close together in the barracks.

We three got to be the best of friends. I would say we formed what we called a triumvirate of comrades. We promised to keep in touch no matter where the war sent us, so if one of us did not come back, the other two would know about it.

There was a graded test every Friday afternoon. However, I had a real problem. I knew nothing about infantry and all their weapons. I did know that second lieutenants were exceedingly apt to become casualties in untold numbers.

I also knew the thinking of these top brass, colonels and lieutenant colonels, was that every soldier there wanted to graduate—get a little gold bar placed on each shoulder, get a short furlough, and then (in my case) off to become cannon fodder. So, what I knew and they did not evidently think about was that I might not want to be a second lieutenant in the infantry. Every soldier there had to pass most of the graded tests, or he would be sent back to his original regular outfit.

As I lay there on my bed at Ft. Benning, I prayed that the Lord would get me out of this trap. He answered by telling me what to do. It came to me very clearly. Every Saturday the names of soldiers taking the test on Friday were posted on the bulletin board with the grades made by each one. My close friends were aghast when they saw what I made on these tests each Friday. These tests were not difficult. A seventh grader could pass them, especially since we studied the material a whole week. I said not a word to anyone about these things.

I flunked every Friday test that I took after getting insight on how to get out of this place. I had to go before a board of colonels to explain why I was failing these tests. They thought I might have problems at home, and if they would give me a short furlough, then I would come back and graduate. I told them a furlough for this reason would not work, and they decided they would try me again.

The test scores got worse, and they called me before the board again and told me they would send me back to my original outfit in Camp Shelby, Mississippi. Was I yellow? Did I have a yellow streak up my spine? I knew I did not and knew self-preservation was the first law of life.

I was called and told to have everything packed and ready to travel at 9:30 A.M., April 16, 1943. A truck picked me up and carried me to Columbus, Georgia, just across the river. My train left there at 9:35 and was to arrive in Birmingham at 6:30 P.M. It would leave Birmingham for Hattiesburg, Mississippi, at 7:00 P.M.

I really think that was one of the happiest days of my life. I had prayed off and on all the way to Birmingham, thankful God had answered my prayers. That evening there was some delay, and I missed my train to Hattiesburg. I ate, got a room, and went to sleep early so I would not miss another train headed south.

The train was very crowded with service men of all branches, but I got on a car with two vivacious young girls sitting together on the backseat. One seat was available on the double seat in front of them. I sat down and pulled all my gear and belongings up beside me. I started talking to these innocents and found out they were Tennessee girls headed for a place in Alabama called York. I was very impressed by one of them as I talked to her. Her name was Reitha Mayberry. I did not tell her then, but I knew she would be my wife in time (if she would accept). She was unusually intelligent, a good conversationalist, and very beautiful!

I told her I was unusually lucky to meet such a girl from Tennessee. I told her when I got to Camp Shelby, I would write her and come to Chattanooga to see her in three weeks when my furlough would start. She just laughed and said, "It's the line all service men use." I asked her for her address and telephone number. She reluctantly gave them to me.

When I reached Camp Shelby, I called Reitha. She was very surprised. In three weeks I did get a furlough, and I rode a Greyhound to Chattanooga. Then, I caught an overloaded bus out to her apartment in Rossville, Georgia. She was on the same bus and did not know it until we both got off the bus. That shows how crowded buses were in 1943.

We visited her parents in Marion County, which adjoins Hamilton County. It was a delightful trip. Her mother was a great cook and the whole family was wonderful. Her parents lived in Sweden's Cove, one of the prettiest places I had ever seen. Springs were flowing out of the sides of the mountain everywhere.

Finally, we went to a great entertainment center called Lake Winnephasuka. Then I proposed to Reitha. She said,

"Yes, I will, but I want to visit your parents in Pensacola, Florida." Reitha had lived in a landlocked state and had never been to the ocean. She saw the ocean for the first time when we visited my parents one month later.

I sent her the best diamond ring I could afford. When one is in the service of his country in wartime, men are moved like checkers on a board. We did not have time to plan a church wedding. We got a minister to marry us in Crewe, Virginia, in Nottaway County, near where Lee surrendered to Grant. It was also the site of Camp Pickett, the staging camp for men going overseas.

Our meeting was no accident or happenstance—this union was a case of divine intervention. It didn't just happen that I missed my train in Birmingham on April 16, 1943. We both knew this from the very beginning. God was leading us daily and still is. We would have celebrated our sixty-first wedding anniversary on December 22, 2004, but Reitha went to be with the Lord on March 1, 2004.

Our wedding date was set for December 22, 1943, and Reitha was to arrive at Camp Pickett about ten days earlier. She had to take a blood test, and it had to go to Richmond and come back to Crewe.

Reitha rode a bus to Blackstone, Virginia, a little town just outside Camp Pickett. When she arrived there, a hard freeze had gripped the area. Places to rent were non-existent. All motels and hotels were booked up for miles around for months.

I met her in Blackstone at 7:15 P.M. What a situation! She was sick. The driver had to stop the bus so she could get out to vomit before she got to Blackstone. We got on a shuttle bus and started to check out Crewe a few miles south of Blackstone to see if we could find a place for her to stay. The bus was very crowded, and I had to stand and hold onto horizontal bars running the length of the bus.

There were two ladies sitting right beside where I was standing (and praying). I overheard one of them tell the other she had been staying in Crewe, but she was heading back to Pennsylvania. The landlady had told her she planned to renovate the room when she left it that morning.

I asked her if she would give me the address of this home in Crewe. She said she would but had nothing to write on. I gave her an old letter from my pocket, and she wrote "609 W. Carolina Ave., Crewe, Va." I thanked her, and when we reached Crewe, there was a large hotel on the main street. It had leather seats around the sides on the lower floor.

We walked into the well-lighted warm lobby of this hotel, and I suggested Reitha stay there while I went to check out 609 West Carolina Avenue. I had faith that if I could see the lady of the house, I could persuade her to let us have that room; if she did not, I would have to go AWOL until I found Reitha a place to stay.

I left the hotel and it was so cold I felt if I touched one of my ears, it would just fall off. Immediately, I found West Carolina Avenue, and now it was a matter of finding 609. I kept walking and I saw a light on a front porch, and there was the number 609.

I rang the doorbell and Mrs. Tucker opened her door. I told her the whole sad story, about Reitha being sick and waiting in the lobby of the hotel. She told me she had planned not to rent any rooms in the upper part of her home because she was going to rework all of them. I told her we were planning to get married December 22, and if she did not let me have a room, I would be forced to go AWOL until I could find Reitha a place to stay.

My plight and my story must have touched her heart. She said, "Under the circumstances, and because you are a sergeant serving our country, I just must let you have one room for your bride-to-be until you are married."

I said, "Praise the Lord—another prayer answered." I ran all the way back to the lobby of the hotel and told Reitha the good news! We gathered all her luggage and set out for 609 West Carolina Avenue. I rang the doorbell again, and the door opened and we walked in. It was so nice and warm in there I hated to leave. When we got Reitha settled in, I returned to camp. Reitha immediately hit it off with this lady. I called the lady from camp and thanked her for her generosity and caring. I then thanked God again for hearing and answering this soldier's request when I was almost in despair.

I woke up the next morning feeling great! Mrs. Tucker told me she always wanted a daughter and now she had one in Reitha. She had two boys, but both were grown, married, and gone. This family was different, so caring and humble—true Virginians.

Reitha needed something to keep her busy while we were waiting to get the blood test back from Richmond. Since Mrs. Tucker had the largest collection of very expensive silver we had ever seen, Reitha shined and polished every piece of that silver for her. Mrs. Tucker fell in love with Reitha, and we never did move until I shipped out and Reitha went back to Chattanooga. We always got a nice letter from the Tuckers every Christmas with a beautiful card until one Christmas we received nothing. We knew our dear friends had gone to their reward.

On our fiftieth wedding anniversary we drove back to Crewe, Virginia, and everything had changed so much, but we found 609 West Carolina Avenue. We knocked on the door, but nobody answered. Dust was thick on everything. We figured it out. The Tuckers' two sons wanted to keep it just like it was. Can't blame them. Their oldest son was in the American Embassy in Saigon; their youngest son was teaching at Vanderbilt in Nashville at that time.

Reitha and I both knew from the outset this marriage was made in heaven. We knew that the Lord was leading step by step, and He always has. We learned to lean on Him. We were always so thankful for the direction we received all those years.

I end this chapter with my dream for the future from Micah 4:3: "And he shall judge among many people, and rebuke strong nations afar off; and they shall beat their swords into plowshares, and their spears into pruning hooks: nation shall not lift up a sword against nation, neither shall they learn war any more." War is inhumane—let's abolish it and take up love instead.

A Soldier's Embarrassing Episode

One day Reitha and I joined another couple as we were window shopping in the little town of Crewe, Virginia. There were so many soldiers on the street all dressed alike that I can very readily see and understand why this embarrassing incident happened the way it did. We stopped at a window that held many onlookers spellbound—some more than others. I happened to be one of the others. My friend's wife happened to be one of the others also. I started walking on down the street thinking Reitha was beside me, but she wasn't. Somebody caught me by the arm as I started walking slowly, and apparently my friend's wife thought she had Marvin, her husband, by the arm. Neither of us noticed until we had walked half a block and I finally noticed I was walking with Marvin's wife instead of mine.

I was shocked, and so was Marvin's wife. Reitha said it was planned. My wife always teased that it was no accident. I laughed and laughed. In a situation like this, what would you have done? The moral of the story is to never take off with just any female holding your arm before checking her out.

A Mess Sergeant:
Everybody's Friend

After searching I have not as yet discovered why the place we assembled and ate was called a mess hall, nor why the sergeant who had the responsibility of food preparation and feeding was called a mess sergeant. All my life I have heard people say, "I'm going to carry my friend a 'mess of turnips.'" I assumed they meant enough for the family's one feeding.

I heard now in this world of change the military has a new name for the place where they assemble and eat—and maybe a new name for the sergeant who has the responsibility of preparing and feeding the troops. That is fine with me, if it is a better term and serves our military personnel. Any sane person is willing to accept change if the change is better. I am not always convinced certain changes are better. I know, however, that some are.

I was a mess sergeant for twenty-eight months while in the Unites States before going overseas. A mess sergeant then was the most popular person in any company or battery because soldiers knew who controlled the food and drinks. Sometimes we had authority to feed certain troops even when it wasn't feeding time. Sometimes a soldier arriving back in the battery from a furlough would ask the mess sergeant for certain favors when it was late at night and he was very hungry. Anyone can see why the troops wanted to be friends with the mess sergeants.

Here is a true incident that happened in our battery during Saturday morning inspection. We were ready. Our shoes were shined, our rifles cleaned, and we were clean, shaven, and had fresh haircuts. We had a barber in our battery, which made it easy for us.

We were all lined up. Each soldier had or was supposed to have had his mess kit clean and ready for the inspection. The colonel started down the first row. Then he started down the second row . . . all was going fine . . . then the third row. Our captain was behind the colonel with his notebook, and behind our captain was our first sergeant.

The first soldier in the third row was a rookie. The colonel looked this soldier over and then looked at his mess kit. The colonel indicated to our captain that this soldier's mess kit wasn't clean. The captain wrote this down and handed the note to the first sergeant. This rookie asked our captain if he could comment to the colonel. He was given permission. Here is what the rookie said, "Sir, if my mess kit is clean enough for me to eat from, it seems to me it ought to be clean enough for somebody else to look at!" We all sighed because we knew the rookie had it coming.

He was restricted to the battery for twenty-one days, plus he had to be on KP (kitchen police) those days. We seemed to agree with the rookie's logic, but he mouthed off to the wrong person at the wrong time, for the wrong reason. These are lessons recruits have to learn or they suffer. I have seen some inspectors who would have laughed about that, but this wasn't one of those.

The Saddest Day of My Life

When I started writing my memoirs, I intended to leave this out. For many years I could not bring myself to even talk about it because it affected me so much emotionally. However, this is part of my autobiography, and it will have to be included.

As a platoon leader, I got very close to the men who made up the squads in my platoon and the men were very close to one another as well. Any one member would have died for anyone else who was in serious trouble on the battlefield, or anywhere else for that matter. The care and love that develop among a group of military comrades is exceedingly strong—"all for one and one for all" describes this well.

In combat, bullets are no respecter of persons—we never know if one has our number on it. In the military we hear lots about friendly fire. It is happening in Afghanistan and Iraq today—seemingly it should be a misnomer, but at the same time, it is a reality.

I understand friendly fire because in the war in 1945, I shot one of my best squad leaders through a tragic mistake. It was with an air-cooled .30-caliber machine gun. The bullet hit this soldier in the fleshy part of the thigh, just missing the bone. It opened up a hole in his thigh into which one could place a fist. We could see the bone. I was so devastated I wanted to die. If I had not had my life anchored in Christ, I would have been a goner for sure.

This squad leader was sent back to Maryland, his home state, and I understand he is still living. The One I'm serving and owe my allegiance to brought me through that terrible disaster. If I could have taken his place, I would have gladly done so. Every member of our platoon knew I was doing all I could, but there are times when things go awry.

Going to War

On March 1, 1944, we shipped out from Newport News, Virginia, making a straight line toward England. However, we made a right-hand turn and headed down toward the Panama Canal. As our ship passed through the canal, there wasn't room to fit a razor blade on either side of us.

When we left the States, we didn't know where we were going, but then it became clear. We passed through the canal into the Pacific Ocean. Our ship was an old Dutch freighter, the *Cota-Inten*, converted to a troop transport. We were on that ship for thirty-seven days and thirty-seven nights.

Only a hundred miles from our first destination in southern New Guinea, on April 10, 1944, we had a dreadful encounter in the Coral Sea. On a moonlit night, no kitchen garbage was to be thrown overboard until after 2 A.M. Two sailors, who thought the rules didn't apply to them, had disobeyed those orders, endangering every life on that transport, including their own.

A Japanese submarine was on our tail. Our captain announced over the speaker system that the submarine was following the floating debris from the refuse thrown overboard from the kitchen. He also told each soldier to grab everything he might want to save and carry it to the top deck. All of the gun tubs were packed with soldiers, so we could not fire even if we had wanted to. Packed like sardines on the top deck, all we could do was wait—and pray.

In three minutes, the two destroyers on each side of us were to release their torpedoes, or tin cans, as we called them. With each can's explosion, the old ship shook and quivered for about three minutes. We were so close to each other, we could feel the heartbeat of the guy next to us.

The man in front of me was Wade Nobles, a big, mean guy from Evergreen, Alabama. His heart was beating as fast as mine. Although I had never seen this man interested in God, Wade said to me, "Keep praying, Clarence! Keep praying!"

I told him, "You pray, too, Wade! God hears a sinner's prayer, no matter where he prays it." He was uttering something, but I don't know if they were religious words or not.

I was so scared, it was as if my heart were in my throat. I had the funniest sensation I have ever had. Then my Savior spoke to me in that moment: "Be not afraid. Over yonder horizon I have a work for you to do." As I heard those words echo in my heart, my eyes searched the actual horizon, wondering what the next few minutes would bring. A soldier is not prepared to fight until he sees something bigger than himself staring him in the face.

Suddenly, the Japanese submarine was destroyed, and the radar went all the way down to zero. We were ordered back to our respective decks, but there was no sleep the rest of that night. The providential hand of God saved us all on that ship. Praise His wonderful name!

We landed in southern New Guinea. It was still raw there, meaning there were still Japanese troops in the immediate area. That first night, I didn't sleep a wink because there were the weirdest sounds coming from the jungle that this farm boy had never heard!

Also during that night, a bullet went through the tent of our first lieutenant. It was either the enemy or what I call a commander's worst nightmare. This man was not liked by the troops, and the next morning he was shipped to another unit.

There we soldiered and trained with troops from Australia. Those men were friendly, but all they wanted was a rifle, two bandoleers of ammo, and time for a pot of tea.

We were put on an Aussie ship for fourteen days going to Hollandia. They had to have their two meals of mutton a day, and the meat was stored in big metal drums. I remember seeing hair on some of the carcasses, and to this day, I cannot abide even the thought of mutton! I lived for fourteen days on black bread and water.

Our first combat was seen at Hollandia. We were then sent to Mindanao, the southern most island of the Philippines. Here we spent the next eleven months fighting the Japanese.

Follow Orders or Die

I fought in the Pacific: two years in New Guinea, in the invasion of Morotai Island, and in the Philippine liberation.

I was wounded twice, but I refused to go to a hospital because my wounds were not severe enough to warrant hospitalization; plus, I did not want to leave my platoon.

We took Morotai Island in southeastern Indonesia Moluccas (Spice Islands) in September 1944. This was directly south of the Philippines. The Japanese saw immediately the handwriting on the wall, so it was do or die for them.

They began with vigor to bomb us off the island—they knew our B24s from there would pulverize the Philippines for the Philippine liberation. Theirs was a night bombing—never came over in daytime because they knew they wouldn't have a chance. We dug in deeply, cut coconut logs, and placed them over the tops of these hasty field fortifications. At night there were no lights—period. Everyone wore his helmet and *never* fastened the chinstrap

Under fire from a Japanese counterattack.

because if the chinstrap were fastened, one's neck would be broken from the bomb's concussions.

Our big searchlights from all sides of the island would start combing the sky as soon as they heard these planes coming. These lights would cross on a plane, and it would look like the midday sun was shining on it. Then large guns would start firing at these bombers. We were ordered not to get out of the bunkers because when a direct hit was made, debris would start raining down—ranging in size from a teakettle to a jeep. It was obey orders or die, and some soldiers died.

On the third day after we invaded Morotai Island, everyone was asleep but me. All of a sudden, I heard a Japanese Zero plane coming straight toward us at treetop level. The pilot was looking for the four howitzers set up to our left in a banana plantation.

I yelled for Claude Pearce, a friend from my hometown of Evergreen and a squad leader, to man the .50-caliber machine gun. I told him to throw up a stream of fire in front of the plane and not to move or stop shooting because if the plane kept its course, it would run right into our line of fire.

The Japanese plane flew right into our trap, the bullets ruptured its gas tank, and black smoke began to pour from the back of the plane as it began to go down into the jungle. We raced to the crash site. The pilot was wearing shorts and a shell fragment hit him in the thigh, severing the femoral artery, so he was dead by the time we arrived. We tried to get a souvenir from the plane, but we had no hacksaw.

Later, Claude painted a red flag on the machine gun to denote it had its first victim on that third day of the invasion. We were ecstatic! We were far from home, but

Clarence (middle) with platoon after the battle. That's a monkey sitting on the gun Pearce used to bring down the Zero.

Clarence with his rifle in camp.

we felt our loved ones were safer with one less Japanese plane in the air.

My job as platoon sergeant was to set up a defense for our battery every time we moved. Having been raised in rural Alabama, I copied the way quail sleep in a circle. These birds sleep heads out, tails in, so that danger from any direction can be detected as soon as possible. We placed the kitchen truck in the middle of a circle of soldiers on guard all around the perimeter with rifles and machine guns. Like the quail, we were able to detect and protect at a moment's notice, thwarting a possible enemy approach while the majority of the men were sleeping.

We were on Morotai Island when President Roosevelt died, and President Truman was sworn in. We won the battle there and shortly after, Leyte was attacked, which was a surprise for the Japanese. The Japanese called General McArthur the Sly Fox. He always landed his troops where the enemy least expected. This saved many lives and it cut enemy lines, leading to the important military strategy of letting them wither on the vine. This helped shorten the war. Believe me that was what we wanted. This is my opinion, and I'm entitled to it because I was there.

The Japanese were expecting the liberation forces to land on Mindanao, the southernmost and second-largest island. Naturally, because of these expectations, this island had lots of men, supplies, and defenses, and was thought ready for the Americans.

The Americans steamed right by Mindanao and hit Leyte. The Japanese were caught off guard. Then, when the Japanese saw what happened, they tried to get many of their forces off Mindanao in ships and sent them to Leyte. The

Clarence, standing at left, with fellow soldiers and two Filipino soldiers.

American navy was just offshore ready and waiting. You can imagine how it turned out—another shortening of the war. President Truman's order to drop the atomic bombs was the straw that broke the camel's back.

I have said nothing about my other friends in the marines, navy, and Seabees. I could not say enough about each one of them if I wrote all day. The marines received some of the most difficult assignments throughout the Pacific campaign (on island-taking and fighting there). A few of those included Guadalcanal, Tarawa, Saipan, and Iwo Jima. The marine dive-bombers once saved us on the Taloma Trail in Mindanao Island.

Our navy's heroes will never be forgotten—they suffered heavy losses, especially during the first part of the war. They were all heroes. Some of my dearest buddies from high school lie below the frigid waters of the North Atlantic due to heavy U-boat activity.

Battle on the Taloma Trail on Mindanao Island.

In the early part of the war, the Seabees were always there (before anybody else had landed many times)—the laying of metal strips to enable our planes to land early meant all the difference for the soldiers. Leveling, removing trees, and constructing the runways helped us so much.

We salute all of you. Airmen, you did a magnificent job, a job that took real men to do. One of my high school buddies, Laula Middleton, was escorting B-17s over Berlin in his P-51 Mustang and was shot down and paid the supreme sacrifice. He always called me Shef. The airport in Evergreen, Alabama, is named Laula Middleton Airport in honor of this brave man.

One day this 1938 class of men and women will have another reunion and roll call. What a day! I'll be able to see and hug everyone. I want to hug and rejoice with those who paid the supreme sacrifice first. My high school principal gave us a pep talk before we all departed on May 28, 1938. He said, "Join up and go get 'em." That we did, nearly 100 percent.

Day is done, gone the sun
From the earth, from the hills, from the sky
All is well, safely rest . . . God is nigh.

Army Slaps for Good Treatment

One aspect I don't like about writing my memoirs is I can't just write about the positive parts of my life; I must include the negative slice of the pie as well. It is all the commingling of life rolled together.

I hold no grudges or hard feelings toward my captain or executive officer at all. To err is human; to forgive is divine. This happened after my division invaded and took Morotai Island directly south of the Philippines. Our first sergeant's wife had cancer of the brain, which was inoperable, and papers reached General McArthur's headquarters outlining this serious situation and the need for our first sergeant to be relieved to return home. This request was granted.

Then, the next oldest and really qualified sergeant in service was made first sergeant. In two months, he returned to the States on the army's then "point system." Now it was my turn to be considered for the topkick position. We had already participated in the Philippine liberation, and the top sergeant position had to be filled at once. I qualified, since I had two years of college completed and was teaching school when we mobilized on November 25, 1940. I had almost had three years in active army training, plus I had three years in the National Guard. Two of those years were serving as platoon sergeant in combat and I was wounded twice.

Who do you think was made first sergeant? He was a nice kid, a draftee I helped train at Camp Shelby, Mississippi. Every member of my platoon was boiling mad and let all the higher-ups know it, too. Honestly, I didn't open my mouth about all of this because the war was winding down, and I knew I was moving on to higher ground quite soon.

Why did he get this rating over me? My entire platoon knew why I had been overlooked: I treated every member just like I would like to be treated. The captain didn't like this! He wanted a slave driver. In so doing, that would make him look great to the majors and lieutenant colonels, and he knew that would boost him right up to major rating. In the army we had a name for this—bucking is one name, but for the sake of modesty I will refrain from using the vulgar term that so accurately describes it. I'm not being envious nor expressing sour grapes, just being truthful.

The Bloodless Surrender

After Japan surrendered, many of their troops, high up in the mountains on the second largest island Mindanao, didn't believe the war was over. Electric lines were laid up into the mountains, and speakers were set up announcing that the war was over. The message in Japanese was to follow the lines down the mountain to the valley where surrender stations were set up. There they would be loaded on Army Ducks (vehicles) that ran on land or in water. The surrender stations were set up as near the stockade as possible. American soldiers there were armed with tommy guns, or grease guns as some called them. They pulled six-hour shifts, and then a new crew came on duty.

The messages in Japanese told the Japanese military to lay down all weapons before reaching the surrender stations or suffer the consequences. The message over the speakers told them they would be protected and carried to a compound at Toril, a little town near Davao, where they would be processed, fed, and in a few days, shipped back to Japan.

This was a great motivator. The enemy soldiers were hesitant at first, but they found out we meant business and each day more and more Japanese came to surrender. We couldn't leave for home (we were told) until they all came down from the mountains. Guess you can imagine how rumors fly in the military!

Japanese prisoners awaiting their trip to the stockade in Toril.

Shipping Home

A memorable day for the whole Thirty-first Dixie Division was November 25, 1945, when we were moved intact from the island of Mindanao to the small town of Toril, twenty miles south of Davao. In advance, we knew the name of the ship that was to take us home—the USS *Charles Carroll*—because Ernie Pyle, a war correspondent in the European Theater, had disembarked from this very ship onto Iwoshima near Okinawa just days before and had been killed a few hours later. His name was written on every bulkhead of that ship.

The war was over. We were jubilant to be going home, so we had a man in a coconut tree with binoculars looking for the ship while the rest of us engaged in a softball game. The lookout saw the ship break over the horizon, saw the name on its bow, and came shouting, "It's here! It's here!"

The game was terminated, the tents immediately torn down, and we packed and went aboard. We were then told where to sleep and more information about the ship that would be our home for the next few days.

Three days out, we encountered a typhoon in the China Sea. Never had we experienced anything like this. When the huge waves hit us, the ship slid in the trough, and everyone had to hold on for dear life or be thrown against the sides of the ship and be killed.

The ship was built for the North Atlantic and had a heavy ballast of steel in its bottom from bow to stern. Our captain, an old seaman, said we must change course, so we went 250 miles out of the way. Even then it was horrific. Had it not been for the heavy ballast, we might have sunk.

Needless to say, there were no unbelievers on this vessel when we reached the calm waters of the Pacific. What the war had not accomplished in changing a soldier's life, the raging water finished. Later the old Dutch ship, the *Cota-Inten*, was sunk near Okinawa by Japanese suicide bombers as she was shuttling troops.

I was very happy the day I was married to Reitha. I was happy the day I finished graduate school at Peabody. I was happy when our two children were born.

There was another day that had an unusual ring of happiness for me. We were returning from overseas' duty on December 7, 1945, just as the sun was rising, exactly four years to the day and hour after Pearl Harbor was bombed. As our ship, USS *Charles Carroll*, slid underneath the Golden Gate Bridge, there were lots of little boats flying Old Glory and girls in shorts waving and playing patriotic music and whistling. I absolutely was so happy and overcome by all this I could not say a word. This was happiness that made me speechless. I didn't say anything until I was in San Francisco Bay near Alcatraz

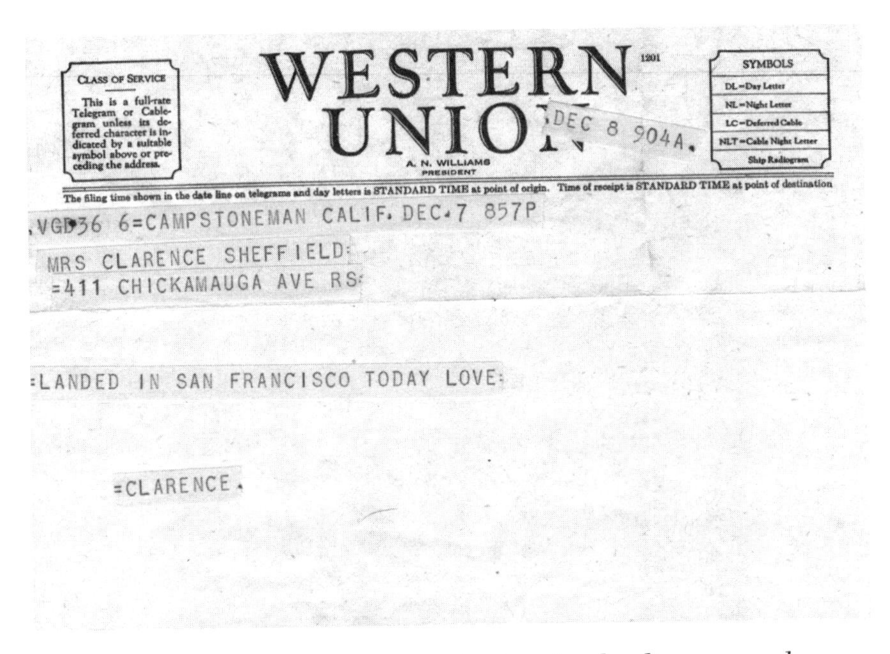
WESTERN UNION

A. N. WILLIAMS
PRESIDENT

CLASS OF SERVICE
This is a full-rate Telegram or Cablegram unless its deferred character is indicated by a suitable symbol above or preceding the address.

SYMBOLS
DL=Day Letter
NL=Night Letter
LC=Deferred Cable
NLT=Cable Night Letter
Ship Radiogram

1201

The filing time shown in the date line on telegrams and day letters is STANDARD TIME at point of origin. Time of receipt is STANDARD TIME at point of destination

DEC 8 904A.

.VGD36 6=CAMPSTONEMAN CALIF. DEC.7 857P

MRS CLARENCE SHEFFIELD:
=411 CHICKAMAUGA AVE RS:

:LANDED IN SAN FRANCISCO TODAY LOVE:

=CLARENCE.

The telegram Clarence sent to Reitha after landing across the San Francisco Bay at Camp Stoneman.

when the seagulls were being fed stale bread. They flew down in great droves and were fighting for this bread. I laughed, and after that I could talk. To be honest, this was the happiest day of my life. If I had been on land at this time, I believe I could have kissed the ground.

A Tribute to a Great General

After being discharged in 1945, I attended the University of Chattanooga for several months but was not happy there. The army told me if I reenlisted for three years, my family and I would be sent to Nuremberg, Germany, for the trials were set to begin. So I reenlisted. However, the army did not live up to its word and sent me everywhere but Germany. I went to Ft. Oglethorpe, Georgia; then to Camp Campbell, Kentucky; then to Ft. Ord, California; and then to Ft. Lewis, Washington. I was there when my daughter Shirley was born.

To be honest, I prayed more in 1946 than ever before or after. I was so discouraged at the army's lack of integrity that I was on the rim of despair. At this point I was transferred to Ft. Bragg, North Carolina. I arrived in the middle of the night and had to catch a taxi to the base.

When I found my barracks, every soldier was asleep and snoring to beat the band. I found a bunk close to the door and lay down but didn't sleep. I prayed, "Lord, You have been with me since I gave You my heart in 1934. I need Your guidance more than ever. Please show me what to do." I prayed like that the rest of the night, while the other men slept peacefully.

Right before first light, the Lord answered my prayers. He spoke to my heart, "At dawn, put on your best uniform. Go outside and look up . . . find the big flag on the hill. Go there and you will find the help you need."

When I went outside, I saw the flag flying high on the hill in front of headquarters. I was tired when I got to the headquarters—and it seemed everyone there was drinking coffee. I know what I'm about to write, every service man or woman living will say is the biggest lie ever told concerning the military. However, *it is true*. My wife, Reitha, was my witness. This could never have happened if the Higher Power had not gone ahead to set the stage. When God goes ahead of us, we will succeed.

I walked up the front steps, opened the door, and a master sergeant sat just inside on the left, drinking coffee. He said, "Can we help you, Sergeant?"

I answered, "Yes, I'd like to speak to the commander of Ft. Bragg."

He replied, "Go on back; he just came in . . . his door is ajar . . . midway back." There was also a major who was drinking coffee, and he directed me back to where the door was ajar.

I went back and knocked on the door and was told to enter—you know the formality, I suppose. I saluted the major general (two stars), and he asked me to sit down. Then I told him my name and why I was there. He really lit up and started asking lots of questions, especially about the Death March. I told him I wasn't on the Death March, but a friend of mine from Chattanooga was on it.

After a long talk, I saw tears in his eyes. He said, "Sergeant, what can I do to help you?"

I said, "Sir, the greatest help right now would be a *long* furlough to help me get it all together. My life is like a 'joint snake'—it all seems to come apart in joints. I need time. I have served my country as a soldier. Now, I want to serve my country as a civilian."

He picked up the phone, then paused, and asked what my company was. I told him—then he proceeded to talk to the first sergeant of the company. He said, "At 5 o'clock this afternoon your clerk should have ready for Sgt. Clarence A. Sheffield a furlough starting today, October 2, 1946, and ending ninety days later."

I jumped up, saluted him, and thanked him so much! I was in a state of happy shock. I could not believe it. Reitha and our one-month-old daughter had a two-room apartment in Fayetteville. I rushed down to tell Reitha the good news. She immediately wanted to board a Greyhound for Chattanooga.

I have tried to find out who was Ft. Bragg's commander on October 2, 1946, and I have failed to find out to date. I don't know whether he is alive or dead—either way, this general helped me, so he will go down in my book as one of the greatest persons I ever met. What a man! What a happy sergeant!

So at 6:30 P.M. that evening, two happy, young, married people were on their way to Chattanooga. There were no freeways then between Fayetteville and Chattanooga. Our route had lots of hairpin curves, and I had to hold Shirley. When we made the curves, the two of us would wind up on the other side of the bus. This went on for miles and miles, and I thought it would never end; but with that ninety-day furlough, I thought I could endure fire I was so happy. I was thinking—Halloween at home, Thanksgiving at home, Christmas at home! I was really on cloud nine, for good reason, too.

On January 2, 1947, I returned to Ft. Bragg. As I was signing in, the clerk walked over to me and told me an order had come down while I was gone: Any soldier who was married could be discharged in two days if he so desired. I said, "Fix me up."

He fixed my papers, and in two days I was discharged. I wish I at least knew the name of that major general. Men like this are what have made America great. Sir, wherever you are, many thanks. This sergeant is striving to meet you up there. I have reason to know where you are.

Part 3

Teaching Years

Payback in Order

Bread tossed on the waters has a way of returning—this is a tribute to my dear wife, a helper in so many ways they simply cannot be enumerated.

My father taught us boys that a clean, virtuous wife and mother is one of God's greatest creations, but a morally loose, degenerate, selfish woman with a vaulting ambition for earthly things is one of the worst of creations. No one is born with such excessive, undesirable traits but is taught by undesirable teachers or parents and associates. I disagree with the sociologist that says, "We are born animals and achieve humanity by associating with people in the group." This is *not* the way I view life at all.

Reitha helped me so much after I was discharged and returned home from the army. At first, it was hard to forget things, and physically I was a wreck. Knowingly, she said, "I would eat bread and drink water before I would spend one dime of the money sent to me to live on by the government." This was a sacrifice for her, and I knew it

Reitha Sheffield.

was from the heart. She proved this by handing me every penny of the money. This was in contrast to what some of my army buddies walked into when they returned.

Our first house was under the "flyway" from Atlanta to Chattanooga. Having lived on the most bombed island in the Pacific for seven months caused me great fear and anxiety (from plane noises) at night. Half asleep at night, all of a sudden I found myself under the bed with cold sweat all over my body. Reitha would talk to me—reassuring me these weren't Japanese planes but friendly planes headed for the Chattanooga airport. Finally, she would convince me to come out.

She was patient and prayed for me as she did the two years I was away fighting the Japanese. Her prayers were answered. Many times during those two years overseas, I was literally in the jaws of death. Thankfully, I had a Deliverer. One reason I'm writing this book is to show all people how faithful our Savior is if we trust and obey Him.

Reitha taught our two children well. Many times as our children were growing up, Reitha would say, "Sometimes I wish we were on a desert island some place"—she was worrying about what Shirley and Wayne were exposed to on the playground and recreational areas that were supposed to be supervised! We finally agreed that we were placed here to help show others a better way and *not* to use some of the language that we heard out there.

Reitha should have been a CPA; she was so apt and efficient in money matters. I never was good in fiscal matters, and her books always checked to the penny. The Lord knew exactly what I needed, and He directed our *doings*. She was also a large-portrait artist for twenty-nine years.

Our first house in Chattanooga bought with a six-thousand-dollar GI loan in 1946.

Also, she helped me tutor and guide the many children we took to our cabin on Lookout Mountain for weekend retreats. She was always willing to go that extra mile to help a child who needed love, instruction, and encouragement that he or she was somebody worthwhile. She qualified for all the verses in the last chapter of Proverbs about a good mother and wife. Today her husband, daughter, son, and son-in-law rise up and call her blessed! “Behind every good, honest, successful man there is a good, honest, praying wife” is also true of her. I have been on elevators when certain women got on and the men would remove their hats. This happened when I was a small boy, and I didn’t understand the meaning and respect this act conveyed. Now, I know.

Why I Was a Jonah

When I started working for National Biscuit Company (NBC) soon after being discharged from the army the second time, all doors seem to swing open almost instantly. There were only two men with college training at this National Biscuit division in Chattanooga. Since the manager planned to retire in eighteen months and I had education, my possibilities for promotion were extremely good.

With such excellent job opportunity, I quickly forgot all about God's perfect will for me. So, it didn't take long for me to be the unhappiest man alive. I hated to go to work because I had run away from God's presence in my life. Therefore, I plunged myself into the social aspects of this new life: boating on Lake Chickamauga, parties, any gathering that would take my mind off of where I was and where I should have been. This put me way out into left field spiritually.

I knew perfectly well I was running away from teaching, because for a man with a family, teaching wasn't lucrative at all after World War II, even for those with a master's degree. With the NBC, I had the chance to make a lot of money to give my family and myself a better life than we had ever hoped for.

So many times we rationalize our behavior so we can look justified in the eyes of our family.

Also, for the previous five years, I had taken orders, went where I was told, and did what I was commanded; I have always functioned best in a structured environment. However, with this new job, I was now involved in the postwar movement of creating a new middle class, and for a poor farm boy who had been on the frontlines of war, the choices were heady and entangling.

However, instead of everything I touched turning into gold, I was facing disaster with the possible loss of my wife and children through divorce. Here I was facing a new enemy: myself. I wrestled with this awhile and began praying for God's guidance. I got down on my knees, asking God to forgive me, and finally got my priorities straightened out.

I said, "Lord, affluence or poverty, sink or swim, I am at the crossroads of my life. Shall I stay in business or go back to teaching?" I immediately got His direction. I must quit the National Biscuit Company for I had chosen the wrong vocation for the wrong reasons.

In business, I was a Jonah. I was seeking happiness, but found it was elusive. It is like grabbing for a cat in a darkened basement at midnight. One grabs and grabs and finally grabs something that is furry and seems like what is wanted. However, I found what I got was a two-toned kitty with a fluid drive—a skunk! Eventually, I realized the only true happiness comes from God and from being obedient to

Him. I finally got those dollar signs out of my eyes that had blinded and shackled me.

For the first time since my discharge from the service, I felt like a bird let out of its cage. Social clubs, yachts, mansions, and fine cars no longer seemed attractive to me. I had a deep-settled peace. Reitha and I thanked God together; our problems seemed to melt away, and we were happy.

The Lord answered my prayer by having my former principal from Annex School in Conecuh County, Alabama, call me right before classes started in the fall of 1947. He said he needed a principal for the Annex School and offered me the job. After being away six years in the army, I told him I would take it.

I moved to northern Alabama. Since I couldn't find housing for my family, Reitha and Shirley remained in Chattanooga. Our second child was due in November. I missed the birth of our son, Stanley Wayne on November 13, 1947. He was born at 5:15 A.M. in a taxicab on the way to Erlanger Hospital. The headline in the *Chattanooga Free Press* read: "Taxi Loses Race with the Stork." Wayne was deprived of oxygen at birth and thus was born with special needs. However, he has to be one of the kindest and most considerate human beings God has created, and I am proud to be his father.

After one year at Annex, I was moved to a large school in Repton, Alabama. I stayed there three years. When the leaders asked me to take over all the schools in Repton, I promised I would return after I had finished my education. I enrolled at Middle Tennessee State College. After I finished my undergraduate degree, I enrolled at George Peabody School of Education in Nashville, Tennessee.

When I finished my master's degree, the city of Chattanooga offered me quite a bit more in salary than

Repton had. The leaders at Repton understood why I would not be returning. I stayed with the Chattanooga school system until I retired June 12, 1977.

As the only male teacher in most of the schools I taught in, I was often discriminated against. The folks who did this meant to show me up, and somehow thought that would make their jobs easier. If these people were alive, I believe they would deny their wrongdoings.

In teaching, I also discovered students that other teachers labeled incorrigible. Those teachers didn't know my philosophy that there were no unmanageable children if one knows how to reach them through love and recognition. This kind of kid was my cup of tea, and God helped me to reach them.

An example of this was in my thirty-eighth year of teaching. I met with this girl labeled incorrigible and asked her many questions. She answered truthfully. She had a story that broke my heart. I told her that I was her teacher now, and we were going to change many things. I told her I loved her and that God loved her. She looked dubious. We agreed that she would let me prove this to her.

Later, this same girl became the wonder student of the whole school because she discovered that some people *did* love her and that treating others kindly paid off. The single worse thing in this world is a child being born into it and never being loved by anyone.

When I left the National Biscuit Company, there was no way of knowing how many lives would be changed by my entering education. When seeking money and status, I had been swallowed up by greed, pride, and covetousness. I am so grateful that the Lord revealed my error.

Life is so brief, like the lilies of the field; death is so certain, and for humans eternity so long. It behooves us to lay up treasures in heaven where neither moth nor rust corrupts, nor where thieves break in and steal as it says in Matthew 6:19.

Here is a little poem, although I don't know the poet. When God joined Reitha and me together, we took this poem's meaning to lead and guide us for all our years together:

Get and Give

Don't be a miser or slave to your gold,
Giving is wiser a thousand fold,
So get and give, get you must if you are to give.
Give you must if you are to live, for getting
Without giving is existence, not living—
So *get* and *give* and *live*.

THE STORY OF JONAH AND THE WHALE AS TOLD BY A FATHER TO HIS SON

By Clarance Sheffield

Get up, Buddy, come here to your Pap, I'll tell you a story, climb up on my lap.
It's better than the story of Esther and Ruth, a little bit fishy, but every bit the truth.
Now listen right good while I tell you the tale, how old Jonah the prophet got caught by the whale.
The whale caught poor Jonah, and bless your dear soul, he not only caught him, he swallowed him whole.
Now a part of my story is awfully sad, it's about a big city that went to the bad.
When the Lord saw those Ninevites with such wicked old ways, "People," He said, "I can't stand them more than forty more days."
So He spoke to old Jonah and said, "Go cry to the wicked old city and tell them that I give them forty more days to get humbled down, and if they don't do it, I'll tear up their town."
Old Jonah heard the Lord speaking, but he said, "No, I'm a true hard-shelled Baptist and I will not go. Those Ninevah people are nothing to me, and I'm against foreign missions, you see."
So he went to Joppa in great haste; he boarded a ship in a different place.
The Lord looked down on the ship and says He, "Old Jonah is fixing to run off from Me."
So He set the wind a-blowing with squawks and squeals; the sea got rowdy and kicked up its heels.
Old Jonah confessed it was caused by his sin, so the crew threw him out and the whale took him in.
The whale said, "Old fellow, don't fret for I'm sent here to take you in out of the wet, and you are going to get punished just right for your sin," so he opened his big mouth, and poor Jonah went in.

It was the funniest sight, Son, that was ever seen, when Jonah rode off in his new submarine.
On a bed of green seaweed the whale tried to rest, he said, "I'm going to sleep while my food, I digest." But he got pretty restless and sorely afraid, for he rumbled inside, while the old prophet prayed.
So you see how God's message to Ninevah lay in the Dead Letter Office three nights and three days; and those Ninevah people couldn't repent for the message of warning to them was mis-sent.
But on the third day the old whale rose up from his bed with his stomach tore up and a pain in his head; He said, "I must get to the air mighty quick, this filthy old sinner is making me sick."
So he winked his big eye and wiggled his tail, then he pulled to the shore to deliver this mail.
When he got to the shore, he looked all around, then vomited old Jonah clean out on the ground.
Old Jonah thanked God for His mercy and grace, then turned to the whale and made a big face. He said, "After three nights and days, old sucker, you found that a good man is mighty hard to keep down."
He stretched himself out with a yawn and a sigh, and lay down in the sun for his clothes to dry.
When he had rested and dried well in the sun, he started to Ninevah most in a run.
He thought how much better his preaching would be, since from Whale Seminary he had a degree.
He arrived in the city about a week late, but he preached from the time he entered the gate.
The whole population repented and prayed, and the great hand of justice and vengeance was stayed.
When you disobey your mother, remember this tale, if you run off from home, look out for the whale.
There's varmints to get you on sea and on land, and a boy can be swallowed lots easier than a man!

Friends Galore

To have lots of friends we must be friendly. People with friends have laid hold of the world's greatest possessions. Each true friend is a gem of great price. To list or enumerate mine would take days . . . so I will tell about only two. First is a boy I became friends with in elementary school. His name is Olan Padgett. We were buddies all through elementary school. We started high school at the same time.

Some may not believe this, but it is true. I bought a pair of trousers from a clothing store one-fourth mile from our school and assumed that the size marked on the trousers was accurate. The next day I wore these trousers to school, and they were too small in the waist. The length was ok, but I was miserable. Olan and I made a deal since we both had one and a half hours before the next class. I asked him if he would walk down to this clothing store and exchange these trousers for a pair two sizes larger in the waist, and I would get in one of the restroom stalls and lock it until he got back.

We both agreed I would be in a predicament if he didn't come back. He told me he would do that and come right back. He did and returned in record time. The trousers fit perfectly, and I was relieved.

I learned something that day. Don't just tell somebody you're his friend—do something nice for that person, and he will know you are his friend. Actions always speak louder than words. Olan and I were both in C Battery 117 FA, mobilized the same day, and went to Camp Blanding, Florida, together. He had a specialty that was needed in Headquarter Company, so he was transferred there—same battalion but different company. We were in the same battles, endured together, and came home on the same ship. So far as I know, he is now operating a large farm near Century, Florida.

Every time we meet, we remember all of those things we did that people don't believe, and we laugh heartily. A good laugh (or a merry heart) doeth good like a medicine, as Proverbs 17:22 notes. It relieves stress, which is a silent killer.

My second friend was a chemistry teacher. We made a very important discovery: teachers had to eat during the summer months, too. As we were both teachers, we worked at a tourist attraction on Lookout Mountain during the summer. We became the best of friends and spent many weekends at our cabin on Lookout Mountain. Reitha and I went there nearly every weekend. His name was William White.

A week before Christmas in 1969, William's wife was driving to (then) Middle Tennessee State College to pick him up and had a head-on collision that killed her instantly. They had five children, the oldest was a girl

Reitha with William White.

sixteen years old, and the youngest was a boy one and a half years old.

William was devastated like I had never witnessed in my life. We had just gotten out for Christmas. He went down to the bank and drew out five hundred dollars, all in one-dollar bills, got a quart of whiskey, and went to Chattanooga's 8th Street early in the evening. He was handing out money to people on the street. What else he became involved in I don't know, but the people beat him up and almost killed him. An ambulance was called and he wound up in a hospital. They patched him up because he was a bloody mess.

The people at the hospital knew if they turned him out on the street he would go back down there, and the people would kill him. A doctor asked him if he had one real friend, and he told the doctor he did, and said, "His name is Clarence Sheffield, and he lives in East Ridge." That doctor looked up my number and called me at 2 A.M. He told me the situation and told me to hurry because if William went back to 8th Street, they would perhaps kill him. I rapidly got on my clothes, and Reitha said she was going with me. I tried to discourage her, but she went with me anyway.

We drove the shortest way to 8th Street. A mob had formed, and we both got out. I approached the mob with both hands in the air, and the mob quietened some. I told them we were there to take my friend away. They stood back, and I said, "Bill, we are going to another part of the city to see what is going on over there."

I led him to our car and put him in the backseat and locked the doors. I didn't tell him we were going home because he would have objected if he knew he were going there. We gave him liquids that would sober him up. Sometime after 4:30 A.M. he went to sleep on his couch. We covered him up and left.

We had both prayed all the way down, and that made a big difference. The Lord never leaves us nor forsakes us. Greater love hath no man than this, that a man lay down his life for his friends. I really hope that this doesn't sound like bragging, but I would do no less for any of my friends.

There is a long story on this. William went to a Baptist church in East Ridge and surrendered his life to Jesus Christ. His life changed drastically. He was teaching an adults' Bible study when he died. Lung cancer lifted him out of his suffering here.

As I think about God bringing friends into our lives, I am reminded of how our daughter Shirley was the nanny to, and then eventually raised, four children, Hal, Julie, Kelly, and Booth. We have always counted them as our adopted grandchildren. I thank God for all the friends He has brought into my life!

Kelly with four of her precious puppies.

Clarence and Reitha's adopted grandchildren. Clockwise from top: Booth, Hal, Kelly, and Julie.

Comradery:

Camaraderie

Comradery is a feeling of oneness, respect, and learning by being put through the same mill, so to speak. This feeling is gained by an entire group's working for one goal; America is a good example. Look on one of your coins—they all contain the (translated) phrase "one out of many." All for one and one for all. During the war, America was united, aroused, patriotic, and praying. With one goal we bombarded heaven with prayer day and night, and those prayers were heard and answered. God is still in the same business.

When I was a teacher in Chattanooga, we had a School Masters Club that met monthly. We always met at Collegedale in north Chattanooga. First, we had a roll call, then prayer, and then a sumptuous meal was served. After plenty of time for eating, the speaker of the day began. After the speaker stopped, an opportunity was always given for individuals to share with the group some significant happening in his or her school since we last met. This was really rich and rewarding. Comradery was not just a

Clarence is seventh from the left on the front row.

word in the dictionary. We saw we had like problems and shared solutions. Once every third month our wives attended with us. Of course, we tried to do our best then to impress them, and usually it worked.

When we moved to Brooksville, Florida, there was an organization of retired teachers. We had retired teachers and administrators from all over the United States. What talent, what new ideas! This was so rich and encouraging. Here, the male teachers who went away to fight for our beloved country had soldier comradery, and this was the greatest, it seemed. The wives of this group switched tables when they saw us getting together at a certain table or tables, reasoning, "We have already heard these war stories and tales."

This was the best group I ever dined with—the most entertaining for sure—and we wound up inviting each other into our homes to exchange our experiences, laugh, and tell jokes. When I announced I was moving to Tennessee, they were sad and so was I. Old soldiers don't cry much, but we just put on a long face "like a horse."

Clarence, first from left in second row, with East Brainerd faculty, 1969–70.

Experience in Elementary Education

One purpose in writing this chapter is to help young people, especially teachers who are molding or leading our children. I have taught in Alabama, Georgia, and Tennessee. Some years were devoted to being an elementary principal, but most of my thirty-seven years were spent doing what I love most—teaching young children and teenagers.

Sometimes long words look like too much of a task for children to master, so some teachers used easy-to-remember sentences or rhymes to help. For instance, the word "geography" looks difficult to spell. It seems much easier to say, "George Eat Old Gray Rat At Poppy's House Yesterday." The first letter of each word spells geography.

To remember how many days are in each month, we learned this rhyme:

Thirty days hath September
April, June, and November.

All the rest have thirty-one,
Except the second month alone
Which has but twenty-eight in fine
Till leap year gives it twenty-nine.

Once you learn these, you never forget them. They stay with you the rest of your life.

It would make me immensely happy if I could give every worthy young person a scholarship to receive an education. In our high-tech world we must treat our children as our most prized possessions; however, they are being short-changed. Here is an example—when I was doing graduate work, we were told that after we earned our master's degrees and forty hours beyond, our salaries would be greatly increased. They told us the truth, and under the GI Bill, thousands across this great country did this soon after World War II.

After twenty-seven years, the president of the United States decided too much money was being spent on education—some said our schools were costing too much. A plan was devised to unload many of the master's-plus-degree teachers. We were offered inducements to retire. These were so enticing that many of this group all over America retired in 1977. *Hold your seats now*. Many of these teachers were replaced with young, untrained teachers, mostly because they could be employed much cheaper.

Inspirational teachers are worth their weight in gold. A teacher not well-trained in leading innocent children is detrimental to those children. Getting well-trained people out of the profession showed how little those trained teachers were valued—it was money or children.

There are four categories of teachers:

1. inspirational teachers
2. superior teachers
3. good teachers
4. mediocre teachers

The inspirational teacher inspires. Jesus was an inspirational teacher. From first grade through six years in college, I can truthfully say I had only six inspirational teachers. They changed my whole way of thinking about why I am here.

As mentioned before, these teachers employed the first one of the four great wishes that motivates all human behavior—recognition. They told me what they saw in me, and they convinced me of it through private sessions. I failed my first encounter with algebra. The next teacher had private talks with me, and I was told next semester I would be in her class. That time I made an A. What made the difference?

This teacher, Miss Moore, helped me see and understand every human being has at least one talent, and some have more. She played up what she saw in me in the way of ability, motivation, and drive. I saw in her a burning desire and happiness when her students excelled, and she didn't stop until she succeeded. When I returned after World War II, I heard Miss Moore had been promoted to her great reward. I could not find her burial spot. I wanted to lay a cross of flowers on her grave and say, "Thank you, Miss Moore! By God's grace I'll see you when my time comes." People like her never die, they live on in the hearts and lives of those they taught. I firmly believe if a teacher is divinely destined, this person will be an inspirational teacher, regardless.

My daughter's first grade teacher had very little training in college preparing her for teaching, but she was gifted with children. I just sat back and was amazed at what I saw. I was her principal. I had to rate her A+.

Now you could say today we have too many students to do this type of inquiry and discover all these things about each child before we do very much teaching. Someone described the students today coming into the classrooms like cattle being loaded through a chute. This is a good picture of the situation many times. Teachers are asked to teach too many students. This is where a lot of our poor showing comes in. Our children are our dearest possessions, and our country must do a better job of preparing our teachers and reducing the number of students assigned to each one.

Inspirational teachers begin by having a heart-to-heart session with each child. If the child has a poor self-image, this is usually the starting place. This kind of teacher has to convince the student that he or she is always available to help, no matter what is needed. Loving and showing interest in a student's personal life and struggles convinces them you are different and you have bonded with them. Love enables the blind to see—don't tell them that you love them, show them by doing some helpful thing for them and encouraging them. Remember this is no easy task.

After testing to find the child's grade level, the sacrifice comes—are you willing to teach or tutor these neglected children after school or on Saturday to bring them up to grade level with the rest of the class? I have done this after having conferences with the parents of these children. My first experience as a teacher after my graduate work involved this. I let the parents know up front I would not take any money for this service. This brought me great satisfaction.

One time, it also brought a blessing to the whole class. One day in late spring while I was in the cafeteria eating, a mother of two boys I tutored rolled a big electric fan in my room and left it. We did not have air-conditioning, and the fan was a God-sent blessing. The greatest part of it all was seeing the expression on these boys' faces when they moved up with the rest of the class. They knew they were just as smart or capable as the others.

I retired June 12, 1977, after working in public education first as an elementary principal and then as a teacher of children and youth. I started out in Alabama in the fall of 1947 as principal. Finally, I was promoted to teaching where I knew I wanted to be and where the perfect will of God led me.

The Superior Teacher Demonstrates

Superior teachers teach by demonstration! These teachers are the ones to motivate their students most highly. Nearly all subjects can be motivated by use of music, physical education, math, and skits. This type of teacher requires lots of equipment. My wife always told her friends, "Clarence carried everything to school, except the cook-stove." She was almost right, too.

Here is one example in science. I said to students—"Did you ever hear Mother or Father at the filling station say to the man at the station to put thirty-five pounds of air in each tire? What did that mean? Can we weigh air? Today we will find out. Here is a tire on this table with no air in it." I called two strong boys to come up, take this pump, and start pumping up this tire. One of the boys had a tire gauge in his hand. They stopped occasionally and checked with the tire gauge—when thirty-five pounds was reached, they stopped.

Then I told all to watch the teacher take a magic marker and draw one square inch on the hand or arm—what is a square inch? What geometric form is this? Some child knew it's a rectangle. I'd say, "If we did this all over the body, we would have lots of square inches, would we not? At sea level there is fifteen pounds of air pressure approximately pushing on every square inch of our body—that is why we remain erect. The air pressure is equal all over (on all sides). Inside the tire the boys pumped air in until there was thirty-five pounds of air pushing outward, thirty-five pounds on each square inch on the inside of the tire." See, a superior teacher *demonstrates*!

Teachers who use this teaching method should ask for a volunteer pupil to come and tell all what was done in this lesson. The teacher should have some little reward for the pupil who gets all the details right. It doesn't have to be a tangible reward; it could be applause for this pupil.

Do you think Mother and Dad will learn about this lesson tonight? Yes, you are right. A superior teacher has been at work. This method can be adapted in teaching math, grammar, or spelling. One must be creative and make learning a challenge. This kind of teaching travels in the community like wild fire!

The good teacher also *explains*. For example, in science again, we discuss air pressure. I'd have two or three hard-boiled eggs and an old-fashioned milk bottle. While holding the egg where all can see, I'd ask if we can put one of the eggs in this bottle without tearing up the egg. They were all eyes, and hands went up to volunteer in the experiment. I'd take a wadded-up piece of dry paper, light the paper, and let it get burning well before dropping the lighted paper into the bottom of the bottle. Then I'd pause for a few seconds and then place the little end of the egg into the mouth of the milk bottle—the egg went right in with a "thump" sound. Now, I'd ask if we could get the egg out without tearing the egg into little pieces. I'd hold the bottle up over my head and wiggle the bottle until the little end of the egg is in the mouth of the bottle. I'd place the bottle over my head, place my mouth directly under the egg in the mouth of the bottle, and blow hard here while holding the bottle in a vertical position—the air enters the bottle on all sides of the egg, so I'd blow hard! This increases the air pressure on the inside of the bottle, and the egg was pushed out. Of course, I'd be sure all the eggs were *hard-boiled*!

A good teacher explains! Did these lessons go home? They surely did, plus a lot of learning and understanding. A teacher using these kinds of lessons would also receive great status in the community.

The mediocre teacher *tells*. We don't like to admit it, but we have many teachers in this category for various and sundry reasons. First, it is the easiest way to "chalk up" a day, get in a car, and go home. Most teachers in this category will not make lesson plans before facing the children. I know there are far more class interruptions today that interrupt teachers' plans, but it is no excuse for not having plans for the day.

When I was a sophomore at Daphne State, I had a great teacher named Marie D. Swedalis. Her hair was white as snow, and she had a critical eye. There was a certain form every prospective teacher had to follow. At the upper left top of the form was the name and date. At the upper right was a place for Mrs. Swedalis's initials.

Everyone preparing to teach had to have the required number of lesson plans approved and her initials in the upper right-hand corner.

My first two or three lesson plans got no further than the part called motivation, which started the lesson plan. She called me in and told me lots of things about children I did not know! My motivation was not sufficient, neither was it motivating. When she ended her talk with this fellow, I felt as if I ought to just go home. She ended her talk by saying if the children aren't motivated properly, one is fishing in a tub.

That last sentence stuck with me. Many times a category four teacher, a mediocre one, has no plan for the lesson, and he or she resorts to teaching unrelated facts, which are of no interest or not relevant to what the student thinks he or she should be learning. Often sheets are handed out to them to fill in the right word (multiple choice); this has very little value except it keeps the students quiet and busy until the bell rings.

Remember, the first three categories represent most teachers in American classrooms. I believe our young teachers will rise to solve the greatest problem facing America today—education. Our president is right—the education of our children should be our number one concern.

This century could go down as the greatest century in American history if we really decide our job is to educate with less paperwork, fewer boring meetings, and more participation from parents. These are their children and many will gladly join the crusade to advance our achievements, so there will be no country on earth that will match it. We must. We don't have any alternatives. If we work at learning like the men and women work at trying to compete in the Olympics, we can do just that. The largest room in any school in the United States is the room for improvement. Let's do it! Then, we will not be fishing in a tub.

Frequently teachers make or break themselves in the classroom the first two days. This is why a lot of teachers quit the first week. Here's some advice for new teachers: don't dress like the students. Be pleasant and smile and have a plan for each lesson. Have the lessons well organized. Let them know right away you are there to help them but that *you are the top authority in the room*! Learning and enlightenment are the goals, not entertainment.

Here is a true story to illustrate and prove that what I am saying is true and workable. In the fall of 1974, I transferred to a new school. The teachers' names were in the papers days ahead. My first morning to this new school, I got in a gridlock due to a wreck on the street, so I was about ten minutes late. This gave the youngsters a chance to devise a plan to see what they were in for this school term. They asked a little boy named Tony to stand just inside the door. The door was closed, and everyone was seated and very quiet when I opened the door. Tony bowed low and said, "Good morning, Clarence." I looked at the little fellow and put my left hand on his shoulder and with my right palm open gave him a pop on his buttocks, and I said, "My name is Mr. Sheffield. It was the same yesterday and will be Mr. Sheffield the last day of school." Then I sat him down. Then I looked at the rest of the class and asked if they understood what I was saying. You could have heard a pin fall and bounce three times.

Just before Christmas Tony learned they were to move to a new school on the edge of a large lake. His mother called one night and said, "I don't know what I am going to do with Tony; he cries every night." I asked her if she had asked Tony why he was upset. She said, "Yes, Tony doesn't want to leave you."

Children want direction, love, and recognition. This was one of the best years that I ever taught. My light spanking was more symbolic than physical. God gave everybody five senses, and some he gave two more—common and horse. Sometimes we need all seven. May I ask you a question? What would have been the result if I had not acted the way I did that morning? Knowing what to do and doing it are two different things.

The great principle of teaching is absolutely essential if we intend to succeed. Disequilibrium is a part of this principle and means thrown off balance. If one stumbles and cannot immediately regain his balance, he is in a state of disequilibrium until he knows he is not going to fall. When we are satisfied that we aren't going to fall, then we have gained our equilibrium. Before that we are in a state of disequilibrium. This principle of teaching is stated thus—create within the organism (student) that state of disequilibrium. This must not go on for days. Maybe the first day is enough. If this goes on for days, some might say goodbye as I did in my plane geometry class. We can't teach them when they are not there.

Why this principle? Without some of this, the pupil or student decides right away this class is a snap. He concludes, "I have made it in this class," thus motivation is lost and leads to his misbehaving and becoming a wise guy or problem child. Let them know right away you are the teacher and the final authority. Notice I am not saying boss. The students must know right away who the final authority is in the class. When the teacher lets everyone know this, he or she gains respect and is ready to teach. The fear of the Lord is the beginning of knowledge. This is not fear, as we know it. It is awe, respect, and it is necessary at first.

Must Be Told

I taught sixth grade in east Chattanooga. Some would say this is a rough part of town—not really, just a different locality with different problems. On one side we had Billy Goat Hill—many of these children came into the world illegitimately. This disturbed me at first, but I went overboard for these trying to be father and friend as well as a teacher and tutor. I loved these children deeply.

On the other side we had a low-income housing project that was very poor socially and economically. Three blocks down the street was a junior high school. I taught a boy named Jerry; his father was a minister. Jerry had already decided in his mind what awaited him when he enrolled at this junior high.

Jerry came to me because he was fearful of what some of the bullies at this school would do to him when school started. He said, "Mr. Sheffield, tell me what I should do when the bullying starts?"

I said, "Jerry, with such a situation, I recommend this: Look the guy right in the eyes and don't take your eyes off him and say, 'I love you and God loves you, too,' and keep looking the guy right in the eyes while you pause in silence."

He did this the first week of the fall term. After school one evening Jerry came to see his former teacher. He said, "Mr. Sheffield, it worked! It worked!"

"Tell me about it, Jerry."

He said the guy was so shocked, he never said one word. He stood there, and his color changed some, and after some more silence he turned and walked away, not uttering a word.

I felt directed by a Higher Power to say what I did to this young boy. Well, news travels. One day, Jerry's father saw me and said, "Congratulations!" (This is the part I like to write because I felt *so* unworthy.) "Jerry's seventh grade social studies' teacher gave each of the students a clean sheet of paper and told them to write on this sheet of paper the names of three persons they considered to be the greatest in the United States of America. On Jerry's paper your name was one of the three, and I thought you would like to know about it."

That was the reason Jerry's father wanted to congratulate me. I was shocked and humbled to tears. I drove home and pulled into the basement garage and stopped. I thanked God and asked him to never let me say or do anything that would ever hurt my relationship or cause a student of mine to stumble or lose faith in me—James 3:1 tells me that as a teacher, if I cause a child to stumble or lead one down the wrong road, my punishment will be greater than others.

Why I Love America

Having grown up on a farm during the Depression and having been rocked in the cradle of adversity, I gained an appreciation for much that my country has done for me that lots of people take for granted. Being a southern Alabama youth and acquainted with few opportunities to have nice clothes for dressing up like the upper crust flaunted, I tended to feel inferior—especially when I wanted to date and did not have a nice car to take her out nor the clothes that looked chic, which elevates the ego.

This was in America and I was in south Alabama. Some jokingly would say, "What good thing ever came out of Alabama?" I had a burning desire to escape the vicious social strata that existed at the time. When I rode a school bus fourteen miles round trip to the nearest town, some living there looked at me as a country bumpkin, meaning I was a person inferior to them.

My seventh grade teacher was a brilliant lady who helped me greatly to set my goals and helped influence my thinking about why I was on this earth—what our purpose should be and what our attitude toward people who were different from us should be. She was really an inspirational teacher. She whetted my appetite to give it all I had.

Education, all I could get, was my goal. However, there was a real problem: I had no money. I started praying that the Lord would make a way. That prayer was answered through the country that I loved. When I finished high school, I went to a two-year normal school where I worked at the school, and this money paid my tuition and book supplies. Had it not been for this money, I never could have entered college. There is no way I could have gone where I have and done what I have done without the opportunity given by my government. I will be forever grateful for this. I hate to think where I would be today if America had not given me this opportunity.

During the war, provisions were made again to further my education—the GI Bill afforded four more years of college—one year of college paid for every year in service.

I never drew one check of unemployment compensation after being discharged from the army. Reitha and I applied for a GI loan to buy our first house in Chattanooga, Tennessee. After government officials checked my army record in World War II, the loan was granted. But we had to first put down some earnest money. We didn't have enough for this.

We prayed, and Reitha asked me to come with her to a bank in Rossville, Georgia, where she had worked while I was overseas fighting the Japanese. She drew out every penny of the money our government sent her while I was away two years in New Guinea, Morotai Island, and the Philippine liberation. She handed the money to me and said,

"Now, let's thank God for it. He provided it for us." This cemented our relationship as nothing else did.

I summarize here why I love America. My country enabled me to enter college by giving me the opportunity to work and pay for my books and tuition. When the war was over, my country gave me four years of free schooling at Middle Tennessee State College and I graduated in May 1950 as a four-year graduate. My graduate work was completed at George Peabody College in August 1951 with a master's degree. In all, I finished six years of college work, and it happened because my beloved country gave me an opportunity to pursue my education—believe me, it has paid great dividends.

Where there is a will, there is a way—thank God! The way seems dismal sometimes for us, but if we will set our goals high, work hard, and not let discouragement get us down, a new day will dawn for us. Believe me, if we struggle and do not give up, we will forever be grateful. We will then make mothers and fathers very happy indeed. Many educators have said it, "When a person knows where he or she is going, the world steps aside."

Yes, I love my country because our home front acted heroically and united at a time when those of us were manning the guns and trying desperately to deal Japan a deathblow. They backed us 100 percent. We have been called a sleeping giant by many people around the world. We were attacked by Japan December 7, 1941, at Pearl Harbor. President Roosevelt declared America as an arsenal of democracy.

When all our people learned the deceit and treachery Japan was trying to use on us even in Washington at the very time of their planned attack, America was stunned but motivated and moved to action as never before in the history of our republic. Women joined up in the army as WACS (Women's Army Corps), in the navy as WAVES (Women Accepted for Volunteer Emergency Service), and many others joined the marines and other branches of the military to do clerical duties that would have taken a man that was needed on the front lines. This action by the women showed their patriotism and love for our country. This was a smart move and strengthened us greatly and will never be forgotten. It raised our morale and enthusiasm to go "Get 'em." That we did. I've heard enthusiasm means "God within." That would fit for sure.

Men and women left many of our farms and took jobs in shipyards and factories making rations and ammunition of every conceivable caliber. Much time and effort was put into the development of long-range bombers like the B-29. There seemed to be no decrease in shipbuilding. Our people were buying many war bonds.

Men who were fighting greatly appreciated what the home front was doing. Any army moves forward on its stomach and must have guns, clothes, and medicine as well. Our home front deserves an A+ for what they did. Many of us said, "How could we lose when an aroused nation was praying and working like that?" Every single person who worked and prayed on our home front during World War II is a real hero. Never has there been a time when America did so much for so many!

Again, this is another reason I love America. I am an old man now, and the end for me is not far off. General McArthur said, "Old soldiers never die—just fade away." We are reminded that over one thousand of our World War II service men and women are departing this life every day. We are passing the torch to another generation that is highly intelligent and capable to lead our beloved country to great heights and accomplishments. We stand on the threshold of the greatest century in America's history if only we would examine ourselves and straighten out our individual priorities.

When the century ends, it will not matter how much money we have stashed away in some bank, the sort of house we lived in, or the kind of car we drove, but that the world may be different because we were important in the life of some person, and we determined to make our dreams come true as we marched beneath the rainbow and shouted, "Thank God for such a land as this!"

Hear me, young people, please! Never let our country get in the military state it was in when the Japanese bombed Pearl Harbor, December 7, 1941. The price of freedom is eternal vigilance. I honor and respect my beloved America—the Land of the Free and the Home of the Brave. May Old Glory forever fly as we pay honor to the greatest land of promise in the world! America! We salute you! God Bless America! I love America.

Why a Cabin on the Mountain

While I was teaching at Harrison Elementary on Chickamauga Lake, a friend called to say that his cabin in Mentone, Alabama, on Lookout Mountain was for sale. In the early fifties, we had stayed in this cabin for free and had told our friend if he ever sold the place to let us know first.

Alabama—words fail when I try to explain Mentone, Alabama—quiet, tranquil, serene, majestic, and spiritually embellished beyond words. I had long dreamed of a way to reach unloved and abused children, so I got an idea. Reitha loved my idea, too, so we began to pray. The more we prayed, the more we realized the Lord's leading.

I drove to Ft. Payne, Alabama, one Saturday to see if I could borrow some money to close the deal. We had some money but not enough. I walked into a federal bank there and asked to speak to the president. I greeted the man, stated my business, and he replied, "Mister, we don't want any more business! We have more than we need right now!"

The Sheffields' cabin on the mountain in Mentone, Alabama.

Wow! When I realized this bank president was a pessimist, I shifted gears. After I talked to him a long while, the man went to the back of the bank for some reason, and I overheard another man ask him if he was going to loan me the money. The president replied, "He is the most persistent man I ever saw, so I guess I will. I can't get rid of him!"

I prayed, "Thank you, dear Jesus!" I got the money and bought the cabin before the sun set that day in May 1968.

Although our friend had called it a cabin, it was more than that—three bedrooms, a long living room with sliding glass windows on one side, a stone fireplace, and a long, screened front porch. There was a well drilled eight inches in diameter through fifty-two feet of rock. We drew water out with a hand-cranked windlass with a thirty-six-inch antique water bucket.

Once we bought the place, we started assembling the things we needed to care for the children who would come. We would bring children from my class at school—girls first with Reitha and some of the mothers from Friday nights until Sunday nights.

The next weekend the fathers would do the same with me. We would set up pup tents for sleeping, although the boys wouldn't sleep much the first night, and would cook our food back at the cabin. We took the boys on a cave exploring trip, where we found hundreds of ponchos left on the cave floor by the hippies living there—until they heard our entrance!

I was a spelunker—one who studies and explores caves. I taught the boys that the dripping of water made some of the gigantic formations as large as a tower. As the water evaporated, the little bit of mineral was deposited. We learned a piece of this beautiful mineral the size of a marshmallow is formed in approximately one hundred years.

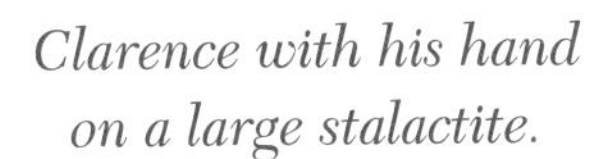

Clarence with his hand on a large stalactite.

The boys were fascinated! They also learned that stalactites stick *tight* to the ceiling; stalagmites *might* reach the roof of the cave if time lasts long enough and there is enough dripping water and evaporation taking place. Then, when the stalagmites and the stalactites join, they form a fluted column.

The boys learned that many caves have waterfalls deep inside the mountain. In time, this creates huge chambers as the water falling erodes or carves out huge rooms that have been given names such as temples, underground sanctuaries, and coliseums. Many of these have perfect acoustics, and this encourages some groups to sing and worship in these chambers; some folks have even said their marriage vows there!

When we would go on a guided tour of a cave, the lights would be turned off for five to six seconds, and we would be in total darkness. Once, just before the lights were turned on, a wife said, "This is the first time Herschel has kissed me in six years!" When the lights were turned back on, she found out that it was not Herschel—evidently she moved out of her place. Sounds like it might have been planned. I guess we'll never know.

The boys were also fascinated to learn that the only animal found in caves that can survive in total darkness is the eyeless, carnivorous salamander. No plant life can survive because plants need to have some sun to live.

When I was a little boy, I saw two mules whose eyeballs were white. When I asked my father about this, he explained that these mules were used in a coal mine too long, making them go blind. Likewise, trapped in a cave, people would go blind in time if not found and taken to the surface where light can stimulate their eyes.

We would take both boys and girls to a cave called Sequoia just off old Highway 11. Sequoia was the Cherokee educator who would teach his pupils in this cave. His alphabet is still visible on the walls there.

Both the boys and girls loved coming to our cabin on the mountain because they knew they were loved and accepted there. These many years later, we have seen some of my former students and without exception they remark, "Mr. Sheffield, my weekend trip to your cabin on Lookout Mountain was one of the highlights of my whole life in elementary school. Thanks to you and your wife!"

Another group Reitha and I took to the cabin was troubled boys from my school. Many had never wet a hook in their lives! We took them to trout farms, put bait on their hooks, and watched them as they caught their first fish. What a joy!

Do you think those boys ever caused anymore trouble or were disruptive in class anymore after that trip? Never—they felt accepted, loved, and recognized—that is what all children need.

During my teaching days at Chattanooga, sometimes we would have heavy snows and schools would be closed. Our family would head for the cabin. Before we reached our destination, we would go down a lane lined with trees on both sides of the road. Down a narrow driveway we would have to stop to crawl under trees and push through undergrowth to get into the cabin. Hard to believe now we did all this! We hiked many times in snow almost waist high. The Lord blessed us so much in those days, and He is still in the same business.

Lookout Mountain is unique in the world in this way: geologists say there are two mountains in the world in which below each is a gigantic underground lake in which no water can get out, and hence all water and snow can do is rise to the surface. There are springs on the surface of Lookout—many of them. The other mountain is in Turkey.

A hotel in Mentone was built in 1848 and is on the highest point on the southern part of Lookout. All the water used in this hotel for years came from a spring on the grounds.

At Mentone, one enters a canyon that runs twenty-two miles. What cut this canyon? It is the biggest canyon east of the Mississippi River. Some say the Tennessee River ran down through Alabama in the far off geological past and cut this canyon. We don't know, for sure, and we are not going to speculate on things that simply puzzle us. We will leave it at that.

PART 4

In Retirement

A Pearl of Great Price

After five years on Lookout Mountain, we started looking for a place to retire. We found a place in Panama City, Florida, and spent some winters there. The seafood was what we liked, for it reminded us of New Orleans. The beaches were some of the finest we had seen.

However, one morning we awoke to see all the palm trees covered in ice. This episode of nature told us we had to go farther south—so we did. We were praying and asking the Lord to lead us to the place where we could be of service to His kingdom and grow spiritually.

He certainly did answer this prayer. We knew some people who lived in Brooksville, Florida—ten miles west of I-75 and forty miles north of Tampa on the west coast. The night we arrived we knew nothing except we were hungry as bears. After searching awhile, we found a restaurant and a little motel on the same street. Neither looked too appealing, but we were so tired and road weary, we stayed.

Front and back views of the Sheffields' home in Wesleyan Village.

Next morning we found the place we were looking for—Wesleyan Village, a short distance from where we spent the night. We found our friends, and the next thing we knew, we bought a trailer!

It was a De-Luxe trailer—it had everything in it and was very nice. There was only one problem. It was like life in a submarine—you had to get permission to pass. However, after a month, we traded it in for a mobile home, and then we had plenty of room.

We got interested in going out into the citrus groves and picking fruit. This was early 1983. There were hundreds of acres in every direction of citrus fruit. The old timers laughed at us and told us how to pick citrus. They told us not to hold the fruit and pull toward your body. Instead, hold the fruit and give a twist—and the fruit comes right off.

The first Sunday we were anxious to go to worship services. We went in a tropical downpour. It literally was pouring down so hard, three men had their shoes off and pants rolled up above their knees and were sweeping water that was pouring in a northwest door beside the auditorium.

We were in that auditorium, and there was a little lady teaching a Sunday school class. Neither of us had ever heard anything like this before. Her name was Ruby Reisdorph. She was a retired missionary, and, with her husband, had been in nearly all the countries of the world. The Spirit so touched everybody in the auditorium that morning that it was wonderful and amazing. People didn't have their eyes glued on the men sweeping out the water. That morning we were conscious that we had found the pearl of great price.

We found out that in the late fifties or early sixties, four or five godly men and their wives prayed, and God gave them a vision and a mission here in a cow pasture east of

Clarence surrounded with his fruit crop on back porch.

Brooksville cemetery. They met, prayed, and God revealed to them what to do here.

It was a struggle at first, but they worked diligently to build a godly village of retirees. There were to be no children unless handicapped. Everyone had to be at least fifty-two years old and retired. If one were not a believer, he or she had to state that he/she would honestly be a seeker if admitted to the village. All had to be approved by the board.

Twenty-five percent could be from other denominations than Wesleyan. No solicitation of any kind, no pets, no alcoholic beverages, no motorcycles, and no loud music or boisterous behavior were allowed. All had to abide by the rules or were asked to leave.

In the early days of Wesleyan Village, the inability to find water almost caused the leaders to abandon the work they had begun. They were drilling near Jasmine Drive without any success. They had drilled deeper than anyone thought possible without striking water.

Then, the godly men prayed. One of them went to the drillers and said they were drilling in the wrong place. He asked them to pull up the drill and then directed them to the new spot. After drilling down normal depth, they struck a large underground stream. Some called it an underground river, and it was running westward. It is thought that this underground stream that runs underneath Wesleyan Village surfaces on the edge of Highway 19 and gives Hernando County a mermaid attraction for tourists.

Part of the village was called Missionary Row, for those retired missionaries who had served in many parts of the

Reitha and Clarence.

Clarence and Reitha at their fiftieth wedding anniversary celebration with John and Shirley Green and Wayne.

world. Their love, service, and dedication to serving God were such a blessing and encouragement to everyone. It was not possible to live in this Village without edification taking place in one's life. This was different than what we were used to. It sounded like the front porch of New Jerusalem, and we found out there was a close correlation. There were talented people who were believers, especially musicians.

However, everything can't remain utopian and after eighteen years, we had to leave a host of friends—hundreds—and this is hard on old people.

On April 8, 2001, we left Wesleyan Village because of the poor health of my wife. Our daughter Shirley and her husband John Green converted their garage into an apartment for us. Shirley is a nurse, and I desperately needed her to help me take care of Reitha. I believe it is Shirley's care that allowed Reitha to live as long as she did.

Now I pick up pictorial directories made during those eighteen years at Wesleyan Village and count the deceased. Over three hundred have already crossed the River. These people die easily—just stop breathing and close their eyes with that angelic look on their faces. Funerals there were so different for the most part—crying and mourning seemed out of place.

My thoughts and prayers go back to the Village and our dear friends who are some of America's cream of the crop. It is always a pleasure to live among people who believe and practice the Golden Rule. May God continue to guide and bless you.

My life has been, as the song so adequately puts it—"The Wonder of It All." The Sheffield clan taught us to strive to live in such a way that when we are gone, it can be said that the world is a better place to live than before. I have been in the very jaws of death many times, but the One I trusted in 1934 saw me through it all. He alone is worthy! The Rose of Sharon—the Good Shepherd—the Lily of the Valley—the Fairest of Ten Thousand to my soul.

Shelter in the Time of Storm

Many Americans seem to blame God when disaster strikes. I heard it immediately after Pearl Harbor and again after September 11, 2001. Who was in command, or who flew the planes into the World Trade Center and Pentagon? For sure God didn't do it. It was the prince of the air (Satan) in the driver's seat September 11, early in the morning. Evil is always around and doing his horrendous deeds when people listen to him.

God will take what was meant for evil and use it for good. This very moment there is overwhelming evidence of this everywhere we look. For example, look how quickly Congress forgot all political bickering and lined up with our president and his cabinet. Church attendance rose, patriotic songs were sung, people were loving one another, and Old Glory was displayed along our streets and homes. People began to turn back to what America has been in the past. Our liberal America (everything goes) had been shaken and shaken hard.

You might say to me, "Didn't you question God about your son being brain damaged at birth?" Yes, I did, but *listen*. No man ever sees the same river twice. I am not the same man I was in 1947 and 1948. The water in the river is not the same; the banks are not the same. I am different now. Hopefully, I have been edified by my faith, and I know (now) everything works together for good to those who love the Lord.

The greatest ally any people can have is the Lord. If we have Him in our hearts and minds and are serving Him, things will turn out right. Our nation has faced madmen as leaders before. How did those fights turn out? Even when it doesn't seem like it, God's hands are always in all human affairs. I believe in referring to my Maker as God or Jesus. I highly resent the phrase, "man upstairs," and other phrases like it because they fail to acknowledge God's involvement in the earth. O God, Thou are worthy!

Our nation is long overdue in giving up the hedonistic philosophy of life—seeking pleasure as the number one priority in living. Since the storm in New York, Washington, and Pennsylvania, aren't you thrilled by a nation that is once again turning to God, to the One who is really in control, One who knows the future, the One whose desire is that all should come to Him and none perish? What a joy to see the unity, observe the patriotism, and hear the media mention the need for prayer. My prayer is that this spirit of love and cooperation and godly sharing live beyond this crisis. We shall overcome because God is on our side.

I pray almost constantly that God will give our president and vice president the knowledge and wisdom of Solomon to do the hardest job in the world and lead us in the right paths. Down through the sands of time when the righteous rule, people rejoice; when the sinful rule, the people mourn.

War is inhumanity to man . . . and I have a dream.

> And He shall judge among
> many people and rebuke
> strong nations afar off; and
> they shall beat their swords
> into plowshares, and their
> spears into pruning hooks:
> nation shall not lift up a
> sword against nation,
> neither shall they learn
> war any more (Mic. 4:3).

Can we imagine the lion and the lamb lying down together!

My Sunday school teacher once asked me, "Would you take arms again since you are getting old if your country needed you to defend our homeland and our people?"

"I would." I would be a traitor if I had said no. Civilizations rise; civilizations fall. A certain historian said that all civilizations follow a certain pattern:

(1) From bondage to spiritual faith
(2) From spiritual faith to great courage
(3) From great courage to liberty
(4) From liberty to abundance
(5) From abundance to apathy
(6) From apathy to dependence
(7) From dependence once again to bondage

American civilization is at stages five and six.

When I was younger I read an old book called *The Seven Seeds of Decay*. In it I found that all the empires of earliest times followed this pattern. I am not an alarmist. I love America. I only want what is best for our children and nation.

Since 9/11, our hearts have been stirred; our emotions took a beating by this worst tragedy in American history. We must not speculate, lest we be treading on forbidden territory. With God's hands underneath, our prayers, our donation of blood, our sharing with them of material possessions, we are going to overcome this national tragedy. People of New York, Washington, Virginia, and Pennsylvania, I salute you! You are a great and strong people. May God's everlasting hands be underneath you, sustain you, and help you through this bereavement.

We Americans who witnessed the horror of the terrible destruction on September 11, 2001, just cannot fathom or take in the infamy that was thrust upon us that day. We still have strong emotions about all of this. When we have these roller coaster emotions, we just have to take shelter from the storm in God's providential care. He has promised us this care and protection.

The bravery of so many of the firefighters exhibited during the storm of tragedy will *never, never* be forgotten! The world took notice. "Greater love hath no man than this, that a man lay down his life for his friends" (John 15:33). Those brave souls were and are in our prayers constantly. We will survive this tragedy and rise up to abolish hate and install love. May this blessing be reached in the twenty-first century.

America is united, aroused, and ready to sacrifice and fight! Those offshoot radicals of hate don't know what they have in store for them! Pray, pray, and pray. We *all* are in this thing together. With God's help, we *will* win! God bless America!

My wife and I were in several hurricanes during our eighteen years in Florida. Once a furious hurricane was headed directly toward us in the Gulf of Mexico—thousands were praying, "Lord, shelter us in time of this storm." Sometime during the night, this hurricane turned completely around and headed toward the Yucatan peninsula. Nobody could explain this. It happened.

We saw and read in the paper that Bin Ladin's followers got life sentences without parole for bombings in Tanzania and Kenya, plus they must pay large sums of money to the families who lost their lives in those bombings. They must also pay twenty-six million dollars to the federal government. (I'm using the figures I saw in my daily paper.)

There is an all-seeing eye watching every mortal on earth. There are *always* penalties for wrongdoing. The wheels of justice may grind slowly, but they grind exceedingly fine.

Empty-Nest Syndrome

The empty-nest syndrome hits hard and is most severe for parents with few children whose birthdays are relatively close together. This started for us the Sunday we took our only daughter to a college campus and left her. Something hit us with a whammy that Sunday I will never forget nor adequately explain.

When we finally adjusted to this and were living in Brooksville, Florida, our only son, Wayne, came to me one day and said, "Dad, it's time for me to leave now." My wife was sick a lot then. He could start working where our daughter was employed, so what could we say about the situation? He left, but he left behind two people who really had a hard time dealing with the empty nest. When meals were prepared, three plates were put on the table and one had to be taken up. Many times when a meal was prepared, I would look in his room to find if he were ready.

I guess what hit the two of us most was the fact that he was our prayer partner. Many times Reitha said she would

Clarence and Wayne.

have been dead years before if it had not been for our son praying for her. He has been not only a blessing to Mother, Dad, Shirley, and John, but to hundreds of people where he has worked all these years. He has a tender heart for all people who are hurting and need a friend.

For example, one night we did not put the lid on our metal garbage can. It was empty except for some black soil or charcoal in the bottom. It was beside a post, and a mouse evidently jumped from the post into the can. Wayne was to take care of the garbage cans. A light rain fell that night, and the mouse ran around in this wet muck in the bottom of the can until Wayne found him the next morning.

He was so awestruck, he ran to tell Mother the sad mouse story. Mother said, "Wayne, did you kill it?"

Stanley Wayne Sheffield.

Wayne and Reitha.

He said, "Mother, he looked so pitiful, wet, black all over with *something*; I just could not hurt the poor fellow, and I turned the can over and he ran away." Two generations with different ideas, but Wayne has the tenderest heart of almost anyone I know, so the mouse went free that day!

It is little things like this we missed so much as our nest became empty. Children's words and actions bring much life and joy and really make a house a home.

A Miracle of Miracles

Our son was a teenager when we lived in Stanley Heights in Chattanooga, Tennessee. As one would expect, Wayne had a bicycle and was very active. He seemed to always throw caution to the wind, especially while riding on the bicycle. This event happened on a Friday afternoon about 3:40 P.M. I was on the Ridge Road between East Chattanooga where I had just finished the week of school and was expecting to head for the hills as soon as I got home and picked up Reitha, Wayne, and some provisions. Midway I received a message that my son had been hit by a motorist in East Ridge (Stanley Heights), and they couldn't tell me anything more.

I was stunned and shaken, but I had to get myself together. Reitha and I both got to the scene at the same time and I said, "O God, my son!" He was in a ditch with blood all over his face. At this time, the ambulance came, scooped Wayne up, and told Reitha and me to follow them to the hospital.

The ambulance crew left the scene, but some stayed to detain the teenager involved and take pictures of the scene where Bowling Street crossed Albamarye. This teenager lived on the Albamarye Street directly behind where we lived. His father was an attorney and a good friend of ours.

I requested at the hospital that lots of X rays be made. I didn't want a hurried-up job. They complied. Listen to this: Wayne's head had gone through the windshield, knocking out about 75 percent of the glass, and the impact sent his body about thirty feet over one edge of a large ditch. On first sight, I just knew Wayne would be a basket case. Yet the only thing the doctors could find that required any attention at all was a cut on the left side of his head requiring eight or nine stitches. We stayed at the hospital until all was clear, and then we brought him home.

We went over the scene very closely and found out Wayne ran a stop sign which was at the end of Bowling Street and the teenager could not stop in time since he was not expecting anyone to miss the stop sign. The boy's father agreed to pay all the expenses, but after we both saw how and why it happened, we agreed that it was not his son's fault, and we paid all the expenses, which weren't a lot in 1966.

Wayne learned his lesson well and the hard way. Reitha and I knew the hand of the Lord was on him that evening as we always prayed in our daily devotions, "Lord, protect our children." I hope I never forget my roots and get so sophisticated or high and mighty that I forget I am a little handful of clay to be used by the heavenly Potter.

Reitha's Testimonial at Moon Lake

February 16, 1979, Reitha had a day off, and we both went to the social security office in Chattanooga to get some answers. I had already retired in 1977 from teaching, and she was fifteen months short of having thirty years for full retirement. I took a job with Olan Mills on Carter Street at the photo finishing plant in downtown Chattanooga, working where she worked.

We came home at 5:45 P.M. She complained of pain in her chest. She could not lie down or sit because the pain was so severe. I quickly called her doctor, and he told me to take Reitha to the nearest hospital. He said, "Go now." The nearest hospital was Hutcheson Memorial in Ft. Oglethorpe, Georgia, less than three miles away.

We left right then. The doctors started working with Reitha immediately. After working with her about an hour, one doctor thought I could take her back home, but her doctor had gotten there by this time and he would not allow this. They admitted her, and she seemed to be resting. Several doctors told me to go back home and rest. At this point, I returned home. At 11:30 P.M., her doctor called me and told me to come back to the hospital. Reitha had three cardiac arrests after I left the hospital. Several doctors and nurses brought her out of the cardiac arrests, but she was in critical condition as they moved her to the Intensive Care Unit, or the ICU. She was in ICU, best I remember, fifteen days. In those days they kept cardiac patients much longer than they do now.

The doctors gave me no assurance she would live or ever overcome this tragic episode. Wayne, my son, prayed almost around the clock. He begged the Lord to help his mother, that he needed her desperately—"Don't let my mother die." He was on one side of the bed, and I was on the other side, kneeling. We poured out our hearts to God for healing.

We had already sold our home in Stanley Heights in East Ridge. My daughter Shirley and friends from her extended family in Nashville, Tennessee, had moved us to our retirement home in Mentone, Alabama, on Lookout Mountain. They moved us lock, stock, and barrel—that means nothing was left for us to move or put a hand on. That is love in action.

Living in Mentone, we had joined Moon Lake Baptist Church which had what we called a prayer roll. It covered approximately six hundred people in seven states, and our prayers were compounded. We literally bombarded heaven in requests for Reitha.

It was touch-and-go for Reitha for about one month. Finally, I had to make a move. My daughter, Shirley, told me to bring her to Nashville—to St. Thomas Hospital. I didn't know whether I would get there in time or not, but I did exactly what Shirley told me to do. I made it to St. Thomas Hospital in record time.

Reitha was admitted on Sunday, and later tests revealed she was having a heart attack during that time. On Tuesday morning she was scheduled for an arteriogram (today it is called a heart catheterization). She was hooked up to this machine that looked somewhat like a TV set.

On Monday, she had an unusual experience. She had an odd feeling of warm sensations that started in her throat and moved down through her body to her feet. She then had no more pain and felt like she didn't need to be in a hospital.

Tuesday at 9:00 A.M. two doctors started the arteriogram. These men watched very closely, and from their facial expressions they didn't see what they expected to see, but they continued to the end. They seemed to be befuddled or in a state of confusion because as Dr. John Dixon explained later, the damage to Reitha's heart reversed itself as they were doing the test!

The doctors ran the test a second time from beginning to end to verify the lack of damage. It showed nothing again. Dr. Dixon, recognizing the name of the admitting doctor in the hospital in Ft. Oglethorpe, called to verify Reitha's cardiac diagnosis because he couldn't explain the lack of damage this new test revealed. The doctor in Georgia told him they had the right lady who had had three damaging cardiac arrests on February 16, 1979.

Now, they were really confused and just had no explanation to give Reitha. Dr. Dixon said that sometimes things happen in medicine that mortals just cannot explain, and this was definitely one of those times because her heart looked like it belonged in the chest of an eighteen-year-old.

Reitha said, "Dr. Dixon, you don't have to explain it to me. I know exactly what happened to me—the Lord healed my heart." Dr. Dixon said not a word but walked over to a window, put both hands behind him, and stood there in this position looking out. Then, Dr. Dixon walked out of the room, not uttering a word to anybody.

The next day Reitha was discharged, and happily we drove back to Lookout Mountain and Mentone, praising the Lord! Several months later, Dr. Dixon explained that this experience changed his life. News like this travels in a small town like a dry forest ablaze in a stiff wind. The many people who were holding her up and praying for Reitha also spread it about.

Our pastor was a true soldier of the cross and had a double dose of spiritual discernment. He would always back off what the bulletin said he should preach when the Holy Spirit was nudging to go another way. Our pastor designated a Sunday and asked Reitha if she would give her testimony of what the Lord had done for her. She replied, "Yes, I will tell what the Lord has done for me." We both agreed on a certain Sunday service, and all the prayer partners outside the community were invited.

News circulated in the community about what was to take place. The building was packed and chairs brought in and filled the two sides next to the windows. The center aisle was filled also. Some were praying that firemen would not come by for an inspection!

The first song was, "Heaven Came Down and Glory Filled My Soul." The pianist, a nineteen-year-old girl, suddenly stopped playing on the second verse, jumped off the piano stool, and had a spiritual spell of shouting, an unusual event for a Baptist church.

After she stopped shouting, she gave a ringing testimony. Then Brother Steele said, "Come on up, Reitha, and stand behind the podium and bring your husband to stand there beside you—the whole service is yours. Close out the way the Spirit leads you."

We did. I was facing the audience, and if there was a dry eye in the audience, I didn't see it. Some wept openly. We were told Reitha didn't leave a stone unturned. The preacher knew, and I knew, it was an "Amazing Grace" story. As she finished, the altar filled first, and everywhere people could move a chair out of the way, people were kneeling.

A ninety-two-year-old man was on his face, asking God to restore him since he was out of church after being saved years before. Reitha and I knew he was one of the wealthiest men on Lookout Mountain. He owned seven hundred acres on the mountain and lived in a very modest frame house. He got with the treasurer of the church, and the two figured how much he owed as his back tithe. He wrote a check and gave it to the treasurer before he left the church.

There were many converts and many restored. Lots of young people gave their hearts to Jesus. After a few years, people would stand and tell of their experience of grace and God's great love, mentioning that great day in 1979 when a little lady was bold enough to tell what Jesus did for her.

Before her death, Reitha told me I had to include another example of how we saw God's hand during our time in Mentone. When we moved there, we united with a church and started helping do the many things a church usually does. A young couple from Pennsylvania, missionaries with the Children's Bible Mission, was sent to our community to work. They had two young adopted children, one boy and one girl. A retired couple had a vacant house in Mentone. This couple lived in Birmingham but planned to come back, fix up the old home place, and use it as their retirement home. They told this young couple they could live there for a specified number of months. Then, at the end of this specified time they would have to move. This gave them several months to find a place to live.

They could not find a place. The time was running out, and they had to move out of the house. The church helped them but could not furnish them housing. We had a barn that my two friends and I built in 1979 across a little stream. We walked a foot log to cross the stream. I went to the barn regularly in the mornings to pray. I was praying for this young family, and I sent another SOS to God asking Him to help us solve the problem, which seemed so acute and pressing.

I got the shocker of my life! Immediately, I got this message: "You and yours furnish the housing!" I climbed down from the second floor and walked back to our house. I said to Reitha, "I got a message, but I don't know whether you will like it or not." I told her the message I got.

She said, "I got the same message," so it was confirmed. We bought a very nice mobile home that was secondhand but only a few months old.

Then, we had another problem—where could we put this mobile home? A dear lady owned lots of land on Lookout Mountain. She heard about the problem. She was a widow and a sweet soul. She gave acreage to put the mobile home on. This couple was *so* happy. We all thanked the Lord for His direction and leading. She deeded this couple this land.

This couple told us they would pay us for the home so much every month. We intended it as a gift to them. They paid for the mobile home in half the time they allotted themselves to pay for it.

When the atomic bomb was dropped on two Japanese cities, this soldier believed that it was the greatest power in the universe. How wrong I was! The greatest power in this world is *the power of prayer*!

America:
A Lighthouse in a Storm

Hope springs eternal in the human breast. Freedom is a priceless possession sought by millions of people all over the world. Freedom to many born here is taken for granted; like air until we no longer have it, it becomes the most cherished and sought after commodity on earth.

As we travel and stand on the border between Mexico and the United States, which way are the people headed? Who is trying to get out? Why? Why do whole boatloads of Cubans risk their lives to cross ninety miles of water between Cuba and America? Any sane person knows the answer: it's freedom.

While I was in the Philippine liberation, I heard lots of Filipino people say, "We would give up anything we have to come to America to live where people are free to choose and enjoy life without living under duress."

Before the Berlin Wall came tumbling down, there was no need to have the West guarded; always the needed guards were on the other side (the East side) to keep people from going west. It doesn't take a mathematician to figure this one out. Freedom carries a price tag. The colonists were willing to pay that price. Eternal vigilance. We have a wake-up call now. The world is not the same. We must love our country and be willing to sacrifice our lives if necessary to see it grow, prosper, and be blessed. In God we trust.

No truer words have been written than those on the base of the Statue of Liberty: "A mighty woman with a torch whose flame is the imprisoned lightning, and her name *Mother of Exiles*. From her beacon-hand glows world-wide welcome; her mild eyes command. The air-bridged harbor that twin cities frame. 'Keep ancient lands, your storied pomp,' cries she with silent lips. 'Give me your tired, your poor, your huddled masses, yearning to breathe free, the wretched refuse of your teeming shore. Send these, the homeless, tempest-tossed to me, I lift my lamp beside the golden door!'"

We will need in this twenty-first century to demonstrate love instead of hate. If we rub elbows with peoples of different color, ethnic origins, or races, we can love them and respect them. Even a blind man responds to love. In our world today there's no room for arrogance and a you-are-below-me attitude. We need each other.

The youngsters today are capable of making our country the greatest on earth. The hordes are seeking guidance for their lives. Let's all join hands and hearts as we pray as a nation for the proposition that is put to us in Jeremiah 33:3, "Call unto me, and I will answer thee, and shew thee *great* and *mighty things*, which thou knowest not" (emphasis mine).

The Almighty has a way of reaching hearts, and some have already become *color blind* since September 11 because of a change in heart and mind. These words come from a southern Alabama "redneck" fellow who loves God, country, and *all* people—and is willing to die for it.

Through Difficulty We Rise

In a way, I have avoided this, but I must tell it. Sometimes our humanity tells us one thing, and the Spirit says another. I faced a problem, but after thinking much about what to do (or not to do), the "dos" won over the "don'ts," and so I will try to do what the Spirit nudges me to do.

When the Spirit speaks to us to let us know what is right and what we should do and we ignore it, I believe we grieve the Spirit.

There is a little black man in Brooksville, Florida, who can be seen almost every day on some street holding up a rather large sign to encourage us or warn us. The sign seems large for a small man to hold up hour after hour; the verse on this sign is from the Scriptures. He is always so diligent and faithful every day. One day as I drove by this man, I received a message to my heart. Here was the message—go and get some sandwiches and a drink and bring them to this little man holding up a large sign. Hold up his sign while he eats, drinks, and lets his arms rest.

I ignored this message and I missed a great blessing, plus I grieved the Spirit, which is a bad thing for a Christian to do. Why did I not obey the message? Humanity got in the driver's seat. I knew if I did, in a short time I'd have every reporter come in the area, lots of pictures would be taken, and people would think I just wanted my picture and name to appear in newspapers and on TV. I failed here because I refrained from doing what was right because of what people would be saying.

Excuses like this cause us many times to ignore the inner voice or nudging. I had to repent. Now, my slate is clear and clean. Life is warfare. Satan is busy, but if we pray as we should and read our Bibles daily, God will hold our hands.

In my teaching days in east Chattanooga, it must be truthfully said, more students overcame their difficulties and went out into society as success stories than in any of the other areas I taught. There seemed to be a close correlation between affluence and lethargy—especially during the sixties. Sometimes it seems poverty is a blessing in disguise. It seems paradoxical, and yet is true. Difficulties, such as poverty, often develop our character.

Enthusiasm is a Greek word, which means "God within." Success is all about attitude. Celebrate your successes and find humor in your failures. Don't take yourself so seriously. Loosen up and everyone else will loosen up. Have fun and always show enthusiasm. When all else fails, put on a costume and sing a silly song. Dr. Norman Vincent Peale was right when he said, "I know that very little in the world has been achieved without a big dose of enthusiasm." Regardless of difficulties, hold onto enthusiasm.

I enrolled in a plane geometry class once. The teacher looked as if she had been weaned on sour pickles. I honestly believe if she smiled, she would break her face. My second day concluded my plane geometry for life. I never went back. Attitude and enthusiasm are everything when we are teaching! Teaching and servanthood are twin sisters.

Today, I salute all of you with whom I had the privilege of teaching and doing my best to help you—Godspeed! Hope to meet you over there!

World War II Generation Contrasted to Baby Boomers:

"For all those born before 1945"

We were born before television, penicillin, polio shots, frozen foods, Xerox, plastic contact lenses, Frisbees, and the pill. We were before credit cards, laser beams, and ballpoint pens. Before pantyhose, dishwashers, clothes dryers, electric blankets, air-conditioners, drip-dry clothes, . . . and before man walked on the moon.

We got married first and then lived together. How quaint can you be? In our time, closets were made for clothes not for coming out of. Bunnies were small rabbits, and rabbits were not Volkswagens. Designer jeans were scheming girls named Jean and having a meaningful relationship meant getting along with our cousins.

We thought fast food was what you ate during Lent, and outer space was the back of the Riviera Theatre. We were before househusbands, gay rights, computer dating, dual careers, and commuter marriages. We were before day care centers, group therapy, and nursing homes. We never heard of FM radio, tape decks, electronic typewriters, artificial hearts, word processors, yogurt, and guys wearing earrings. For us, time-sharing meant togetherness . . . not computers nor condominiums. A chip meant a piece of wood. Hardware meant hardware, and software wasn't even a word.

Back then, "Made in Japan" meant junk, and the term "making out" referred to how you did on your exam. Pizzas, McDonald's, and instant coffee were unheard of. We hit the scene when there were five and dime stores where you bought things for five and ten cents. For one nickel you could ride a streetcar, make a phone call, buy a Pepsi or enough stamps to mail one letter and two postcards. You could buy a Chevy coupe for six hundred dollars . . . but who could afford one? A pity, too, because gas was eleven cents a gallon. In our day, grass was mowed, Coke was a cold drink, and pot was something you cooked in. Rock music was grandma's lullaby and aids were helpers in the principal's office. We were certainly not before the differences between the sexes were discovered, but we were surely before the sex change. We made do with what we had. And we were the last generation that was so dumb as to think you needed a husband to have a baby. No wonder we are so confused and there is such a generation gap today. But we survived! What better reason to celebrate?

The Mind

The quality of life is in the mind . . . not in material things. The world is filled with beauty when your heart is filled with love. We grow because we struggle. We learn and we overcome. Goodness is the only investment that never fails. You can plant a dream. Live every day of your life as though you expect to live forever. Don't believe in miracles—depend on them. Kind words do not cost much yet they accomplish much. Cherish yesterday. Dream tomorrow and live today. Be not simply good—but good for something. To desire is to obtain. To aspire is to achieve. Happiness is not pleasure; it is victory. Happiness is very elusive; many don't know from whence it cometh and don't know how to keep it once it is theirs.

Benefits of Too Many Birthdays:

"A Little Mixed Up" (Not me, yet)

Just a line to say I'm living,
That I'm not among the dead.
Though I am getting more forgetful
And mixed up in my head.
I've gotten used to my arthritis.
To my dentures I'm resigned.
I can manage my bifocals.
But, oh God, I miss my mind.
For sometimes I can't remember,
When I stand at the foot of the stairs,
If I should go up for something
Or if I've just come down from there.
And before the refrigerator
Often my mind is filled with doubt.
Have I put food away
Or am I just to take some out?
And there are times when it is dark
With my nightcap on my head,

I don't know if I'm retiring or
Just getting out of bed.
So if it's my time to write you,
There's no time of getting sore.
I may think that I have written you
And don't want to be a bore.
So remember I do love you,
And I do wish you were near.
Now it's nearly mail time,
So I must say goodbye, dear.
There I stood beside the mailbox
With a face so very red.
Instead of mailing you my letter,
I had opened it instead.

Author Unknown

Good Morning, As Well As Adios

I paraphrase some of the Song of Solomon: "For, lo, the winter is past, the rain is over and gone; the flowers appear on the earth; the time of the singing of the birds is come, and the voice of the turtle is heard in our land; the fig tree putteth forth her green figs, and the vines with the tender grape give a sweet smell" (2:11–13a).

Everything must have an end like the beautiful flowers that come up in early spring. I am really trying to tell it like it was, how it is, and how it will be when the moss on my grave marker is so thick it will be hard to read. "I ain't gonna be 'thar' no way." My writing, I hope, will be as unique as my fingerprints. Be lenient with me if I've sounded too moralistic—it is my life and that is the way the cookie has crumbled for eighty-seven years. To God be the glory!

This old soldier must now close the gate. Around me a new day is dawning! Newer things seem to have a brighter luster. The rainbow has Old Glory mixed in it. What a scene for a reunion of our buddies who went away but did not come back like many of us did!

> *I'm not dying, just fading away as I'm entering the Land of Beulah! Sing all, "This is the Land of Beulah!"*
>
> *Adios,*
> *Clarence Sheffield*

About the Author

Clarence Addison Sheffield has been a student, soldier, teacher, husband, and father, among other accomplishments. It was in his pre-college years that he became inspired by great teachers and determined to become one himself. His college education at Daphne State Teachers' College was interrupted by World War II, during which he served in the Pacific.

Discharged from the army in 1947 at the rank of sergeant, Sheffield continued his college career and received a bachelor's degree in education from Middle Tennessee State College (later known as Middle Tennessee State University). He later earned a master's degree from George Peabody College (now part of Vanderbilt University) in Nashville. He also completed additional course work and credits toward a doctorate, which he chose not to pursue due to the economic climate for teachers at the time. In his nearly forty years in education, he taught in elementary schools, as well as served as a principal in schools in Alabama and Georgia.

After retiring from teaching, he moved to Brooksville, Florida, where he served for six years as president of the Retired Teachers Association in Wesleyan Village.

Born near Mt. Union, Alabama, in 1917, Sheffield married Reitha Mayberry in 1943, a union that lasted sixty years. Sheffield currently lives in Nolensville, Tennessee, with his daughter Shirley and son Wayne. This is his first book.